MAGNIFICENT MINDSET

HOW TO START YOUR DAY THE BEST WAY

TARA BEST

DIVINE DESTINY PUBLISHING

Copyright © 2023 by Tara Best and Divine Destiny Publishing

All Rights Reserved. Apart from any fair dealing for the purposes of research or private study, or criticism or review, as permitted under the Copyright, Designs and Patents Act 1988, this publication may only be reproduced, stored or transmitted, in any form or by any means, with the prior permission in writing of the copyright owner, or in the case of the reprographic reproduction in accordance with the terms of licensees issued by the Copyright Licensing Agency. Enquiries concerning reproduction outside those terms should be sent to the publisher.

CONTENTS

PART ONE 1

1. Chapter 1 3
   The Moment My Life Changed Forever
2. Chapter 2 20
   Hitting Rock Bottom & Nearly Losing It All
3. Chapter 3 26
   My Commencement On The Journey Of Growth
4. Chapter 4 34
   Falling into The World Of Mindset Completely By Accident
5. Chapter 5 43
   The Moment When It All Clicked
6. Chapter 6 51
   When I Had The Awareness Of The Power And Potential Of A Morning Routine
7. Chapter 7 59
   How Does Your Mind Function & How Does This Relate To A Morning Routine?
8. Chapter 8 68
   How Can A Morning Routine Help You Deal With The Day?

PART TWO 75

9. Chapter 9 77
   Gratitude
10. Chapter 10 89
    Affirmations
11. Chapter 11 103
    Journaling
12. Chapter 12 112
    Vision Board
13. Chapter 13 121
    Goals
14. Chapter 14 135
    Meditation And Visualisation

PART THREE   143

15. **Chapter 15**   145
    How Can A Morning Routine Improve Your Self-Belief?

16. **Chapter 16**   150
    How Can A Morning Routine Help You Feel More Positive?

17. **Chapter 17**   156
    How Can A Morning Routine Help You Feel Calm and Focused For The Day?

18. **Chapter 18**   160
    How Can A Morning Routine Help You With Your Intention For The Day?

19. **Chapter 19**   164
    How Can A Morning Routine Help You Feel Connected To Your Long-Term Vision?

20. **Chapter 20**   173
    The Varying Lengths And Ways To Do A Morning Routine

21. **Chapter 21**   186
    A Heartfelt Congratulations!

22. **About The Author**   188
    Tara Best

PART ONE

CHAPTER 1

THE MOMENT MY LIFE CHANGED FOREVER

"If you don't ask, you don't get"

Surely, I didn't need 'mindset work'? I certainly didn't need to do a morning routine or add another thing to the list. I was busy enough already. I was confident in what I offered. How on earth was this going to ever help me? I felt like I had hit my earning ceiling, so surely, I just needed more strategies and tips to earn more. That's why I signed up with this coach. Certainly not for 'woo woo' things to add to my list.

That was October 2018. Since then, through mindset work, my life has changed so much, even more than I could have imagined. But the story didn't start there. First, let's rewind a few years.

I'll never forget how miserable, fed up, broke, and sad I felt. I was working a job I greatly disliked. It was late 2014 and I had just finished working my last day before the Christmas break. The next two and a half weeks were mine to spend time with friends and family and to chill out and enjoy not having to go to work every day. I worked in hospitality, so to have that time off over the busy festive period was a dream.

I had graduated from University one year prior, having completed a Bachelor of Science Degree in International Equine & Agricultural Business Management at the prestigious Royal Agricultural College. Yet, I still hadn't found the job or calling that would enable me to utilise that degree and truly light me up.

Since graduating in 2013, I have had two managerial roles in the hospitality sector, each time hoping that the experience I would gain would set me in a good position for future roles. I loved the managerial aspect of my role, running a team, organising advertising features in local publications, managing social media, and marketing and being the face of the establishment. I loved speaking to people, building relationships with customers, and smiling as the regulars would walk through the door, excited to hear their news and updates.

But something was truly lacking, I felt like I lost the love. I felt unappreciated. My creativity and desire were squashed and before long, I dreaded going in.

That Christmas break felt like freedom. It was a taste of what I desired, life on my terms and doing things that light me up. I felt free and joyful once again. I enjoyed each day, spending time with Si, my boyfriend at the time and now my husband, feeling happy and able to just *be*. But as with any break or time off, the day soon arrived when I headed back to work. Monday 5th January rolled around and off I went, feeling somewhat glum. Was it the January, post-Christmas blues? Was it my lack of love for work? My lack of purpose in life? Or a blend of it all? The only shining light of potential joy was a trip we had booked to the Caribbean on the 23rd of January. If I could just get through the next few weeks I'll have freedom again, albeit temporarily.

I realised something had to change. I just didn't know what or how.

I remember those first few weeks of January so clearly. I just felt desperate. Constantly feeling sad and counting down the hours until I could get home and have some wine. I would cry the whole of the 20-minute journey home. It felt like a release, like I'd been holding back the tears all day as I bottled my feelings, not feeling appreciated or worthy and constantly having to justify myself.

Driving home, the tears ran non-stop. They poured so freely down my face as I replayed the events of the day in my mind and remembered how I had been treated. Under-appreciated was the biggest thing. I tried so hard. I had created great relationships with the customers, I knew they enjoyed coming in and spending time chatting with me. I couldn't shake the feeling of just being stuck. I knew I was meant for more. I knew this couldn't be my life. I knew deep down I desired freedom and happiness, but I just didn't know how to get there. I'd get home and just try to block it all out.

Then when driving to work, I was constantly wondering and worrying about what the day might have in store. Whilst at work, I was always worried about what was next, and whilst driving home, I was worried about what the next day would entail. I was in a constant cycle of worry and sadness.

Deep down, I knew my life shouldn't be or feel this way. I had a great partner, Si, great friends, a gorgeous cottage with Si in a stunning Cotswolds village and yet inside, I was miserable. I just felt stuck.

At the time, I was very good at bottling things up. I had, and still have, a wonderful relationship with Si, but I haven't always found it easy to share things when they're going wrong. It's like I need time to process and can then easily talk about something *after* the moment. This will become even more apparent as we go through this book.

So there I was, at the time, feeling so saddened, and yet, I just didn't know what to say. I knew Si would support me regardless, but I didn't know how to explain it. It sounded so silly while whirring around in my mind. The things I was experiencing on a day-to-day basis weren't massive or groundbreaking as individual moments, so I just kept going. I'm a strong woman that can cope with most things, except spiders! It was more the cumulative effect of ALL of the moments over a period of many months that really got to me. The events and instances weren't isolated, it was all building up on top of each other.

After work one day, before going home to Si, I popped in to see my Mum and Sister. I burst into tears at the kitchen table as I shared how deeply upset I was about my job. My younger sister, who ran a successful photography business, told me to just set up my own business. I loved her positivity, yet it just felt so out of reach for me. What on EARTH could I do? I didn't even know what I wanted to do, let alone what I actually could do. My mind was numb to opportunities. I just couldn't think of anything, which again, made me so frustrated.

I remember trying to list out my experience and expertise as well as things I liked to do and just couldn't find a job in it. It didn't feel like an option. Plus, even though I had a business degree, I didn't really know how to start or run a business. Around this time, Twitter and Facebook were the primary social media channels and I don't recall following anyone that I could look up to for inspiration or finding anyone online that I could take advice from. I just felt lost and totally fed up.

Knowing something absolutely had to change, I started applying for any sort of job I could find. I applied for so many random roles just to get out of my current situation. I applied for a job as a secretary and was told I'd get bored too easily. I fancied myself in a sales role as a regional sales agent, yet was told I didn't have any sales experience so that was a no-go. I applied for a role as an equine nutritionist because I had studied it as part of my degree and loved it, yet I was told I didn't do enough of it as part of my degree. I even looked into doing my Accountancy qualifications, but then realised I hated numbers, and it sounded incredibly boring. I even thought about getting a master's degree, thinking it would at least buy me some time and get me on the right track, or at least I prayed it would. But it would cost a lot and be so full-time I wouldn't be able to work alongside it.

I just kept hearing no. Maybe these employers sensed my desperation and didn't want to give me a chance because I was in a bad place mentally. It felt so demoralising. I kept trying. I kept applying. I knew something must stick; I must get a yes at some point. It took real guts to keep showing up and applying for roles with an ounce of optimism when all you're hearing is no, no, no. This was really difficult.

Feeling deflated, I decided to try again after the holiday. Maybe then I'd be refreshed. Or a genius idea would come to me from a Caribbean beach. I hoped and prayed.

Soon enough, it was the night before our trip. There was a lot of weight on my shoulders and I felt physically weighed down. As we finished packing I felt a little bit of the weight release. I hoped and trusted that more would lift as we boarded that 7-hour flight the next day.

The next morning we sat awaiting our flight call in the departure lounge at Heathrow airport, one of my favourite places! We checked in, had a wander around the shops, and enjoyed a light breakfast. I recall sharing with Si about a potential job I wanted to apply for. I had met the business owner the week before and since meeting him and hearing about what his company did, I suddenly felt like this was my calling. I could see myself doing this job. It was working as a Land Agent, managing estates and the countryside. It sounded like the perfect job. The only issue, I didn't have any qualifications or experience. Many of my friends at The Royal Agricultural College had studied this as their degree, but I didn't know anything about it. Even so, I decided to write an email from the departure lounge, showing my interest in the role, and asked if I could please apply upon our return a week later. It felt like a good step in the right direction before we boarded the plane.

I was so confident in my ability to shine in a new job that I was committed to doing whatever it took. We boarded the plane and I felt a tinge of hope. It was a small one, but it was there. Could this be the break I had longed for? Could it be my time?

I thought about it a little more while on that flight, before trying to put all thoughts of work and my future out of my mind for the week of bliss in the sun.

Seven hours later we landed and as I got off the plane. I felt the heat hit me. There really is nothing like that first step off the plane when you feel the warmth on your skin. I smiled, took a deep breath, and breathed in the Caribbean air.

The holiday was total heaven. We stayed in a gorgeous all-inclusive hotel situated right on the beach. It was surrounded by palm trees, pools, and several bars and restaurants. As a beach lover and sun worshipper, I should have felt more like I was in paradise. And to an extent, I did. I loved it. The beaches were beautiful, the sea was warm, and we had some amazing excursions booked. But there was still something lacking within me.

One of those excursions was a spa day on a yacht out in the Caribbean Sea. The yacht took us out into the sea, anchored up, and we then had our treatments followed by refreshments. There are two vivid memories from that day. The first was having a full body massage on the yacht. There was beautiful calming music playing and the sound of the sea gently tapping the side of the vessel. I love the sound of waves breaking on a beach and this sounded so similar. It genuinely was the most luxurious and relaxing vibe. I tried to switch off. I tried to be in the moment and enjoy the lovely massage. I really struggled to switch my mind off and let go of the fear of going back to work.

The next vivid memory was after we had our spa treatments and were allowed to lounge on the deck with our drinks. I laid on a massive beanbag in the sun, with a chilled glass of white wine. I didn't realise it at the time, but Si took a picture of me lying there in the glorious heat while resting my glass of wine on my stomach. I remember the thoughts that were going through my mind. Whenever I look at that picture, I am reminded of and almost transported back to that very moment with that overriding sense of dread of returning to work. I could feel the fear in my body and sadness in my belly. A feeling of letting myself down, of deflation. I just couldn't shake it.

The whole week was overshadowed by the fact I had to return to a job I didn't like when I got back. We had worked so hard to be able to afford and justify that trip and I felt annoyed at myself for the thoughts I was having.

Once the holiday was over, I headed back to work, almost admitting defeat and just giving up my dream and desire for more.

A few months later, while still at that job, I met a local gentleman who had just set up a new business. He mentioned he'd likely be coming in a lot for meetings as he got his business off the ground. I was excited for him and shared that enthusiasm for his new venture. I truly love building relationships, I love speaking to people, finding out their stories, finding out about their goals, and really hearing about what lights them up. That's a trait that has got me to where I am today, but more on that later!

Then a moment happened that changed the trajectory of my life forever...

CHAPTER 1

Being an extremely friendly, interested, and extroverted person, I got chatting with him and asked a little more about the new business he was starting. It turned out he was setting up an equestrian lifestyle website, offering articles, reviews, interviews, and reports. My ears perked up when he mentioned the aim and angle of the business, I had always been a horsey girl! We hit it off immediately and as predicted, he kept coming into my place of work for business meetings. I was always eager to hear more about his progress, the plans he had in place, and what his aims were.

One day, he came in for coffee and as usual we got talking. I jokingly, rather tongue in cheek, offered to write a blog for him. I had always been into horses - my Mum had a pony ready for me before I was even born so it wasn't even up for discussion as to whether or not I'd be a pony-mad little girl! I had loved having ponies and horses throughout my life and I even focused my business degree in this industry.

He kindly agreed to accept a blog from me (hurrah!!) and told me I had free rein on what I wanted to write and to make sure it included something I was passionate about. I had no idea what lay ahead.

I went home that evening, excited to get writing and started immediately. The words just flowed; they came so easily. I truly loved every second. I'll never forget constructing that word document. The buzz, the tingle, and the excitement were unreal.

Could this be it?!

Could this be the calling I so desperately wanted?

I chose to write the blog on retraining racehorses, as it was something I had done before with the help of my Mum and had seen some great success. It was also something I was super passionate about. I love to see the transformation of a retired racehorse, who in their own right are so majestic and athletic. I love to see how they go on to have a wonderful second career and life.

I adored writing that piece. I did my research and shared some of my own experiences and stories. I even got some case studies from local riders who I knew had retrained a racehorse and had success in their chosen discipline. I nervously shared the first draft with my Mum - I've always been fiercely independent and never relied on her for coursework or homework when I was studying. I actually felt a little apprehensive about her feedback but just wanted to see what she thought. To my relief, she said it was great!

Around the same time as I was writing that first blog, which was something I planned to do alongside my place of work, my bosses mentioned that they would be changing my contract.

I was told that I had to work more hours, start earlier, and work every single weekend. The initial pull for that specific managerial role was that I didn't need to work weekends, as I had already had to do that and work every weekend in a previous job. I wanted to enjoy life, I wanted to have some freedom.

So, you can imagine how unappealing the new contract sounded. I was instantly turned off, and then told it would be for no more money. I asked what would happen if I didn't sign the updated contract? They politely said I could leave.

I'll never forget that moment…

THIS WAS IT!!! My escape! The moment I had been waiting for…. Thank you thank you thank you Universe! I couldn't believe my luck. I didn't know anything about 'the universe' at the time, in terms of how it works with you (we'll get into that much more later in the book!). But I knew the stars aligned at that very moment.

The only thing was, I didn't have a single penny of savings, literally, my ISA had £0.00p in it, and I had £200 in my bank account. I had rent to pay, a car on finance, a lot of monthly direct debits, and I liked having, earning, and spending money! Yet strangely, I didn't even think twice about the answer. Not once did I question my decision, I chose to leave. I don't even recall talking through the decision with Si or my Mum. I just knew. This was it. I was so excited! The conversation wasn't even open for discussion. I chose to leave before even thinking about the money or the lack of what I had in my account. Deep down I knew something, or someone was giving me an out. I now realise it was the universe. I told Si my decision, I told my boss my decision, and I was asked to work just a 3-day handover.

The evening of that first day of my 3-day handover, I was due to go and see the gentleman who had asked me to write the blog for him. I had given it to him the week before and he said he loved it, so he asked me to pop in. I went to see him and told him in a rather jovial tone, that in two days I would be unemployed! I don't know if anyone has ever felt so happy about upcoming unemployment. Even typing this now, I can feel the excitement, the opportunities, the joy, the freedom, the everything that I felt back then. It literally makes me smile to this very day.

I think he thought I was joking!

Again, being a confident and extroverted person, I dropped into the conversation that if he needed any more blogs or social media support I would be delighted to help. My life motto ever since that wonderful day has been "if you don't ask, you don't get" - it's so true! I genuinely wouldn't be sitting here writing this or having created what I've created if I didn't follow that motto.

He seemed really keen and told me he would pay me £150 for that first article I had written. I couldn't quite believe it! £150 for an article that I just loved creating. How epic was that! I just couldn't believe my luck.

I worked my 3-day handover and Wednesday 17th June 2015 was my last day of employment. Little did I know at the time, but this was the first day of my most epic life and business journey. At the end of that day, I met the gentleman again at his office. I strutted in, head held high, walking with confidence and a bit of swag, and I sat in one of the leather chairs as I celebrated the fact I was now unemployed. We got on really well and he hinted at some potential work I could do, which was insanely exciting.

As I left that evening and started to drive back to our beautiful cottage, I felt free. I felt light. I felt like I could breathe. I felt buzzy! I've honestly never felt a mix of such excitement and relief in my entire life. I just couldn't believe it was all happening - I literally remember screaming with excitement in my car while the tunes were blaring.

The next few days were just joyous. I was writing a number of articles for my new client, working from our gorgeous, rented cottage, and being my own boss. I just loved writing - who knew that was hiding in me? When I had written my list of what I liked and was good at, writing never came up.

CHAPTER 1

On Thursday of the following week, the phone rang. It was the man I had been writing for. Immediately I felt a tinge of excitement when I answered the phone. He told me with excitement that the website had just gone live for his new business! I felt honoured he wanted to celebrate it with me! He then asked me if I was available and wanted to go to an equestrian event to write for him on Saturday, in just two days.

Let me think about it for a moment. Did I fancy going to one of the world's leading equestrian events as an accredited journalist and writing some articles for him? Ummm yes of course I did!!!! I hung up the phone and felt the excitement coursing through my body. I jumped up and down on the spot and squealed with excitement then rang Si to let him know! I then popped a status on Facebook sharing the news that the website was live and that I was heading to Hickstead on Saturday to write. I rounded off my status by saying *"This is going to be the start of something special..."* I just had no idea how special.

I immediately started packing some things to get ready for the journey. A journey I will never forget.

That Saturday, the 27th of June was another day when my life changed forever. It felt like I had won the lottery. In fact, it felt better than that! I won the lottery of life. I had hope once again that I could be happy, joyous, and have fun in life and work.

It's still a day I celebrate now and one of the proudest moments of my life. It felt like the first day of the rest of my life and is the day I now celebrate as my business anniversary.

I'll never forget that first morning working as a journalist.

I woke up at 5.30 am, pumped, excited, and wondering if this was all for real. I left our home at 6 am to make the 150-mile journey to the event. It was a beautiful Summer morning, the sun rising brightly over the M4 motorway. I couldn't stop smiling. I stopped at a service station for a flat white and chocolate muffin and couldn't help but spread joy as I took the goodies from the barista, wishing her the most amazing day upon my departure. I absolutely adore driving and always have but that drive was one I will never forget. It is one of my happiest moments ever. I smiled the whole way, I had the tunes on, I was singing my heart out and I just felt so grateful for this opportunity. The sun shone brightly the whole way. It felt like the universe was looking down on me, guiding and encouraging me, making this moment as perfect as it could possibly be.

When I arrived at the event, I couldn't believe my luck. It was just fabulous and as an accredited journalist, I had an all-access pass. I followed the signs that directed me to the press car park, which was as close as you could possibly get to the action of the event. I asked the car park attendant for directions to the press office - feeling a little clueless and clearly very much looking like a beginner!

Throughout the day, I just took it all in my stride. I interviewed lots of riders and made lots of notes. I borrowed my sister's spare camera, so I was able to get some photographs to support my report. I genuinely had the most wonderful day. There were moments of 'I don't know what I'm doing' but I just followed my gut. I knew I could work it out. I listened and observed to witness what else was going on. I'm absolutely certain I looked like a beginner, but I tried to keep that thought out of my mind. Everyone has to start somewhere, right?

Where there were breaks in the schedule of what I wanted to watch, I either sat in the press office writing my articles or went for a wander around the shops. It all felt surreal. At lunchtime, I was given a lunch voucher, which could be redeemed at any of the food trucks on site. What a delight that was! I didn't know that food would be included. I went and ordered a duck wrap and enjoyed it while watching some of the competition classes.

The afternoon provided some amazing competition and again, I sat there feeling like I was in a dream. I was in awe of the riders I was watching, taking lots of notes, and texting the owner of the company little snippets so he could put some updates on Facebook and Twitter throughout the day.

It truly was one of the best days of my life and career, and one I truly cherish. It was the big break I had been waiting for. Even writing about it nearly seven and a half years later, I still feel those tingly and excited feelings. It's anchored so deep within me as a day I will never forget.

At about 6 pm, as the show wound to a close, I made my way back to my car. I was shattered, but on such a high. On the journey home, I actually did another scream of excitement in my car - the third I had ever done. It didn't feel real. This perfect job and doing something I immediately and deeply loved felt like a dream.

Very soon after that initial day as a journalist, I started doing the website management for the company I worked for, adding my articles and blogs to the website and before long I was managing their social media too.

Then, my client recommended me to his neighbour, and I started doing her social media management too. She even recommended me to one of her friends. I kept posting on social media, sharing my client's posts, results, and stories, and before long, I had people asking me how they could increase their brand awareness, sales, and get featured in magazines. I had done a little bit of public relations at a previous job, not even knowing that's what it was called at the time. I thought it was just advertising.

So, as with so often in my business, I said yes and then figured it out after.

I had no idea what to charge. I just charged based on what felt right, which I now realise is key when pricing yourself. At that time it was £50 a week for social media management. I was still working as a journalist and had a daily rate of £150, which felt like the best thing in the world. One thing that had been consistent for me during that time, I was showing up on social media. I was constantly putting myself out there, even though I had no idea how to promote myself. I was constantly building relationships, working with my clients, and gaining new work through word of mouth.

I realised over that summer I had gradually started doing less journalism and more marketing, a completely unplanned, unintended pivot. I was still in the bubble of joy with what I was doing. I was loving the work and started to make fairly decent money, bringing in about £3,000-4,000 a month during that busy summer of 2016. In October 2016, I launched my very first website and officially launched Tara Punter PR, my PR and Marketing company.

I was terrified to put it out into the world. I was officially putting myself out there. What would people think? Who was I to set up this company? Was it right? Was it the right name? Did I offer the right things? What if someone called me out and called me a fraud? I was wrapped in fear, but I did it anyway.

At 8 pm it went live, I had a glass of Prosecco and sat next to Si. It was terrifying, but it was a step in the right direction. I shared the link on social media and awaited people to message me about how they could work with me. Yet, nothing happened. Was the website really live? Did the link not work? Why weren't people wanting to work with me?

I genuinely thought it would immediately bring me lots of clients. After all, isn't that the main purpose of a website? Naturally, I felt a little deflated but still celebrated this achievement.

Over the following months, my website did start to drive traffic. I was sharing it regularly. I was producing blogs, and I was consistently posting on social media. It felt like everything was continuing to move in the right direction.

Then in April 2017, I hit a true rock bottom, nearly losing it all.

CHAPTER 2

HITTING ROCK BOTTOM & NEARLY LOSING IT ALL

"You have everything within you to get through whatever life or the Universe throws at you. Literally everything, you've just got to un-lock it."

They say you don't know how lucky you are until you nearly lose it all. April 2017 was that month for me, a month I'll never forget, but for all the wrong reasons. The success I thought I had been living was taken away from me on one fateful day.

It was a Thursday. It started the same as any other, with me going for a ride on my horse, Ollie. Upon returning home and settling into work, I was hit with not one, but two clients going bust on that same day, one of which was my biggest client.

I couldn't believe it.

It crushed me like 1,000 tons of bricks landing on me.

I remember being struck into a panic. How did this happen? How had two clients gone bust in one morning? Was it my fault? I was in charge of their marketing, could I have helped them avoid this? Could I have helped them generate more sales? Will they blame me? Could I have stopped this from happening? At that moment, I felt that I wasn't very good at my job.

Due to the clients going bust, my invoices didn't get paid, and I had thousands of pounds outstanding. Having been living very much month to month, I had no backup plan in terms of finances. No savings, no overflow or overdraft. No credit card, no loan facility. I was screwed. I actually buried my head in the sand a little, something I really don't recommend to anyone. I let my direct debits bounce, I went overdrawn which cost me greatly, and I was just worried the whole time. I was living in a state of fear, panic, and always focusing on the lack of money coming into my life.

When I look back at that time now, I see how my mindset was in the wrong place. Now that I have a strong understanding of the Law of Attraction, mindset and manifestation, I recognise how my focus was totally in the wrong place. I was heavily focused on the lack of money coming into my life and the abundance of bills and letters from the bank. So that's exactly what I kept manifesting. I just didn't see a way out.

I would lay awake for nights on end trying to figure out how I could get out of this mess, but I was in it so deep, and so emotional about it that I just couldn't find a way through. Literally, nothing came to mind as to how I could handle the situation or approach this subject. I hadn't had any training on this as part of my degree and up until that point, I had very much just figured things out for myself. This time, I couldn't.

The severe stress caused by bottling it all up led me to develop stress-induced Irritable Bowel Syndrome (IBS). Initially, I hadn't put the two together. I was in such agony with my stomach pains that I even went to the doctor. They informed me that it was IBS and said that it was due to my diet, with no mention of stress.

Under the doctor's order, I changed my diet. I was keen to see what kept triggering this pain. Yet nothing helped it. It was so painful at times, that I was even apprehensive to eat. It just made it worse. The pain was truly horrendous.

I remember seeing my Mum one day and crying because I was in such pain and so stressed. I told her it felt like I had mini explosions going off in my stomach and she said, "I'm sure it's just the stress of the whole situation." That was the lightbulb moment when I realised this was all caused by stress. It certainly aligned with what had been going on that month. I had never felt or experienced anything like this before. I knew stress wasn't really good for you, but I didn't know why, or what that meant. A quick search on the internet confirmed that yes, IBS can be triggered by stress.

The next day, another letter from the bank dropped through the letterbox, another that I dreaded opening, and I just broke down in tears. At this point, I knew I had to call them.

I rang the number at the top of the letter, my hands shaking, trying to hold it together. As the phone rang, I wondered what I'd even say when someone answered. An employee answered, I held it together for all of three seconds before I just broke down in tears.

CHAPTER 2

The tears wouldn't stop streaming as I tried to explain the situation of why my payments weren't going through and direct debits kept bouncing. Some of the payments had bounced several times. Every time they bounced; I was fined by the bank. The fines alone were racking up along with what I owed on the direct debits and payments themselves.

The gentleman on the phone asked if there was any option for me to get support, perhaps family, friends, or a credit card. I didn't feel there was. I genuinely felt lost and stuck. I was loved and well-supported by friends and family, but I didn't feel like I could ask for help on this level. I had never had an overdraft or a credit card, as I had never trusted myself with it. I felt so helpless. That was the moment I knew I had to tell Si. Before then, I felt so ashamed and just kept thinking I'd figure it out. I had battled alone, hiding the letters, trying to act normal, and just getting on with it. What would he think of me, knowing I had let myself get to this point? And the fact I had kept it from him for so long - I just felt ashamed. Crushed and ashamed.

He came in from the farm one evening and I told him. Again, I burst into tears and explained it all. I don't remember the conversation. I think it was so emotional that I almost blocked it out.

What I do know is this...

As soon as I told him, it felt like the entire weight of the world had been lifted from my shoulders. The second I finished explaining it felt like together, we could conquer the world. I instantly wished I had told him weeks ago. What had I been so afraid of? He reacted so nicely and so full of love and support, of course, why wouldn't he?!

He was so supportive and understanding, and for the first time in our four years together, he bailed me out, and he paid my half of the rent. Without knowing much about gratitude at that time, I felt full of it. Full of gratitude for him, for telling him, for his support, and for the next step. Looking back, I'm so grateful for that time because it gave me the inner strength and resilience to know that I can get through anything life throws at me. Much more on that later.

Almost immediately the pain of the IBS stopped.

Knowing my rent was covered for May, I took action and sorted out the mess I had found myself in. Strangely, as soon as I knew my financial situation was about to get better, my ability to problem solve and have creative inspiration started to flow. I started to think about what I could do or offer next. I still had a couple of social media clients to continue supporting but they paid me £50 a week, which wasn't going to cover my rent let alone anything else, or let me live.

After a few days of thought, I had a realisation. I didn't see a way through this on my own. I barely knew how to run a business, let alone how to bring one back from the ashes. I knew that there was only one thing to fix it.

Months previously, I had met a business coach at a local networking event. Being a small equestrian PR and marketing girl, I didn't think I needed a business coach. I didn't think I was worthy or deserving of one and thought, "who am I to have a business coach?"

I got in touch with her and found out the hour-long session was £97. I could have cried. I didn't have the money. I didn't have any money to spare. There was nothing in my account, I didn't even have money to buy tampons or put fuel in my car. I knew I had to find a way to generate it.

Knowing how well social media worked for me, I did a little post saying I was doing a special offer - a press release written and sent out to the press for just £50. I knew if I could just sell two, I could pay for that session. I sold several and I was able to make that first investment.

Between signing up and attending the in-person session, I had so many fears and limiting beliefs, and so many times I thought about making an excuse not to go and just letting her keep the money. I even thought to say I was ill on that day so I didn't have to go. I recognise now, all of those moments and feelings were because I was stepping outside of my comfort zone and doing something totally alien. I was opening myself and my business up to potential criticism from someone I didn't really know. She didn't know PR; she wasn't equestrian in any way. Was she just going to pick apart everything I knew and had already done? Would she tell me I was wrong to have done 'business' the way I had to that point?

Nervously, I got in the car and started the 40-minute drive to her house.

CHAPTER 3

MY COMMENCEMENT ON THE JOURNEY OF GROWTH

"When was the last time you looked back to see how far you've come?"

I was genuinely terrified when I got to the home of my new coach. That 40-minute car journey to her house felt like one of the longest of my life. I kept coming up with excuses so I could justify why I had done what I had done to this point. Would she see that I'd been blagging it? What would she think of my poor attempt at a business? I can't even begin to tell you some of the negative thoughts that were going through my mind. It felt like I was going to bare my soul. I parked up, got out of the car, and knocked on the door.

. . .

She greeted me, and I entered her home. She instantly made me feel at ease although I was still a little fearful of what might happen or what she might say. I'd never worked with a coach before, I didn't know the protocol, was I meant to have prepared anything?

We sat down in her big open living room and she asked me some carefully crafted questions.

It felt SO nice to be able to open up to someone, without being criticised. I shared how I fell into the world of business, what I did, and the recent struggles I had. I did feel quite ashamed though. I felt that as a 28-year-old, I really should have had a better grip on my life and business and certainly should have had more money in the bank. The way society and social media are currently, there is a really big emphasis on how you *should* live - what you *should* be doing by a certain age, when you *should* be married, when you *should* make £xxx amount by, how many children you *should* have by a certain age, and so on.

As a 28-year-old, who had just gotten engaged, yet was completely broke and didn't even have £97 to invest in my business, I felt like a failure. I didn't have a life plan, but I had always thought I'd be much better off financially by the time I was 30. Which was looking more and more unlikely by the day.

I swallowed my pride for that first session and opened up. I knew I had to be totally honest with this coach if there was any way she was going to help me properly.

We picked apart my business - things I liked, things I didn't, clients, projects, and pricing. It felt really good. I actually felt like a bit of a professional. It felt exciting to plan ahead and think about what I wanted to offer, how I wanted to run my business, and what I wanted to make. Again, nothing I had done to that point. I still have my notes from that first session - It's amazing to look back and see how far you've come in life. Those moments need to be celebrated.

As the session started to draw to a close, we set a goal, the first goal I'd ever set. The goal was £2,500 months. It felt exciting! I must admit, as I packed up my old Dell laptop and scruffy notepad and made my way out to my car, I was a little sad to be leaving. I was surprised to admit I really enjoyed speaking about all things business with someone!

I got in my car to make the 40-minute journey home, very much in an excitable bubble. There was an excited feeling in my stomach again, a tingling that I was pleased wasn't linked to stress or IBS. It felt SO good. It was like a spark had been re-lit. It re-confirmed that I *did* have a good business deep down. I was passionate about what I did, and I wanted to make it work. I just needed help connecting to it and actually implementing a bit of a plan, something I had never done. I had just been going with the flow. I already had some tasks to take action on immediately. On the drive home, I started dreaming about what I wanted for my business.

The £2,500 goal felt SO good but what could be next? Maybe £3,000 or £4,000 a month? *'Gosh that would change my life,'* I thought to myself. I had never earned that much in a month before! That journey home went a lot quicker and was much more enjoyable than the one there!

I got home, put my favourite playlist on, made myself a delicious coffee, got myself a snack, and immediately started on some of the tasks that we discussed. It felt very exhilarating. I was excited to do the work. It was exciting to have some sort of a plan of action and an understanding of what steps were needed to hit my goal. I also really liked the accountability, knowing she would be checking in on my progress. There was no time or space for BS or excuses!

I knew if I didn't do the work I would have to justify and explain why I hadn't. Plus, the only person I'd be letting down is myself. She knew how many, or how few, clients I had and what time I had available. Plus, having paid that £97, I wanted to earn it back! Without even knowing what a growth mindset was, I realise I had one. My next session was in the diary and again, it wasn't "I can't afford this" but rather "how can I afford this?" How could I make that £97 for my next session?

I did a few hours of work and felt truly accomplished. It felt like the work I was doing was important and future-proofing my business. It felt like it had a purpose. I wasn't just wafting around, putting out a tweet on Twitter aimlessly with no real plan or intention.

I had never done work like it - actually working ON not just IN my business. I couldn't wait for Si to get home so I could tell him all about it! He had been running his own successful contracting business for a few years so he knew of the stresses and struggles that come with running a business, and also fully understands the cash flow concerns. I felt like a true grown-up.

When he came home from the farm that night, I felt like a new woman. I shared the exciting plans, what I had been working on, and how lit up and pumped I felt for the future. The weight of the entire world had been lifted.

The only way was up...

Shortly after that first session, I had an enquiry for coaching. One of my followers had asked me to help him get better results on social media. He had seen some of the wins and results that myself and my clients had achieved through using Facebook and Twitter.

As with so many things in business, I said yes, and knew I could figure it out later.

I offered to do an in-person session for £70 which included all preparation for the session, my driving to the client's home in Bristol, 40 minutes away, the session itself, my driving home afterward, and a follow-up call one month later. With the amount of time I put into it, the hourly rate wasn't much better than what I had been earning when I was employed, but I adored it.

It instantly felt like I had found my calling.

The session was amazing! My client had so many lightbulb moments and really seemed so pleased with what we went through and the plan that he had at the end of the session.

After the session, I shared on social media just how much I adored it, along with an amazing testimonial from him. He shared with me that his organic reach on Facebook went from 300 to 30,000 overnight. I was obsessed! I soon had more enquiries for coaching flooding into my inbox.

The results from coaching were amazing. I loved helping business owners of all types with their social media. I helped them to utilise the platforms properly and effectively, and to generate more sales and website traffic. I kept offering in-person power hours to local business owners and drove to their home or office each time.

My business really picked up. By the end of 2017 and into 2018 I continued to be full of dreamy clients, joy, and sales. I loved it! It felt addictive, like I couldn't get enough.

In the Summer of 2018, I had my best sales month ever and I couldn't believe what I had created! I brought in over £6,000 in cash in one month. How could I, the girl that used to hate her job and couldn't work out what she wanted to do, create that in ONE month in a business she adored? It all felt so magical.

I couldn't believe I was making that much money in my own business. It was more than I had ever been paid or earned before. That used to be what I'd earn over 4 months when I was employed.

What made it even greater, was the fact that I adored what I did, and I was helping business owners. I was helping them increase their sales, brand awareness, and actually helping them hit their goals. At this time, I was doing a mix of coaching power hour sessions, as well as managing brands' public relations and social media management. I recall one client exclaiming how thrilled she was that I got her featured in a magazine that she had read since she was a little girl. The job satisfaction was and always has been exceptional. It truly drives me and remains the focus of everything. While I was beyond grateful to have grown my business to a certain level, I still desired more. I wanted to be able to help more people.

As soon as I recognised I wanted more, I couldn't get that hunger and desire out of my mind. It was all I could think about. If I could get such great results with my current repertoire of clients, how epic would it feel to be able to help more? I just felt so ready. I think that's really important to feel ready. So often we spend time comparing ourselves or our journey to others, and feeling like we *should* be growing our sales, or doing more, without actually asking and questioning whether it's what we want and are ready for. The fact I couldn't get it out of my thoughts confirmed my decision.

In August 2018, I mentioned this desire to my coach, who I had been with for a year, and it surprised me that she recommended I work with *her* coach. That felt like a massive step up, so I checked her out online and agreed to have a complimentary chat with her.

As soon as I found her online, I felt hooked by her content. Her energy was infectious, her smile was bold and the success she had created was enviable. I couldn't get enough. I watched every single video she had ever done. I listened to podcasts she was interviewed on. I stalked her social media and got super excited every time I saw a new post or piece of content pop up online. I became obsessed with her message and how she showed up. To me, that was a telling sign that she was the one for me.

I booked a complimentary discovery call to see how she might be able to help me. I hadn't even heard of a discovery call before reaching out to her, so I had absolutely no idea what to expect.

As a girl from The Cotswolds with what felt like a relatively small business, with big dreams, I looked forward to our call date in September. Just like the first meeting with my initial coach, the 'who am I' thoughts crept back in. Who was I to work with a coach of such International success? Having done my research, I knew she was a bit of a jet setter, having lived all around the world, and currently living in South Africa. She charged multiple 5 figures for her 12-month group mastermind and clearly had a no-BS approach to business. Would she even accept me? Would I be worthy of her programme? Would it be a massive mistake if I invested that money?

What if I invested all that money and it was the wrong thing? I didn't even have the money for the 12-month investment. I just kept battling my thoughts right up until the day of the call.

The zoom link came through that morning. At our scheduled time, I pressed the link for the Zoom call. This was the first Zoom call I had ever been on and I was terrified. Yet it would be one of the most pivotal moments of my business and one I am forever grateful for taking.

CHAPTER 4

FALLING INTO THE WORLD OF MINDSET COMPLETELY BY ACCIDENT

"You can have anything you want in this life if you put your mind to it and are willing to do the work."—Karen, my Mum

So there I was, on a Zoom call with a multi-7-figure business owner. A fellow brown-haired, British-born business coach. She was tall, bubbly, and infectious. She had a nice tan, a lovely smile, and gave me every single ounce of her attention. I felt instantly hooked, and a little starstruck! Her energy kept me engrossed from the second I said hello. The call was magnetising. I could feel her energy through the Zoom, it inspired me instantly.

I explained my business to her and mentioned the joy I got from coaching business owners to help them hit their goals and create their dream business. I had shared that I wanted to hit 6 figures in my own business. This was a massive deal for me. I had very rarely heard of a £100k goal so it felt huge, but it also felt exciting and possible, so I clung to those feelings like they were all I had.

During our call, we spoke about pricing, packages, and marketing. Then she asked me a question I didn't think she would. She asked what my email marketing strategy looked like.

I didn't have one. I didn't even have a mailing list. As a self-confessed hater of technology, the thought of setting one up terrified me. I had been in business for over three years at that point, and I really was starting to have big goals for 2019 and beyond. But the truth was, I didn't actually have an email list, I just had my social media followers. I felt shameful admitting that. What sort of business owner didn't have an email list? Did it make me a failure? *Should* I have had one by now? Would I have had more sales by now if I had one? How did it look if a PR & Marketing expert didn't have an email list, an integral part of a marketing strategy?

Instantly the imposter syndrome, self-doubt, and 'who am I' thoughts and fears rose to the surface.

We mapped out what I learnt to be called 'a freebie' on that call and she gave me some pointers on how to set up an email marketing platform and automating this freebie to get sent as soon as anyone signs up for my mailing list. I fully committed to doing this after the call.

There was so much value in that call and many probing questions - things that really got me thinking. It made me realise I had actually done well to get to where I was, but that it truly had all been blagged. Even with the support I had received from my first coach, it still felt like there was an element of blagging. I remember thinking to myself, "imagine if I actually had a strategy, a plan, or a coach from the start, anything could have been possible!"

But it still was…

The value-packed 60-minute call left me feeling so pumped and unstoppable. I felt so ready to work with her. But, while I felt so ready to go to the next step and so excited to start, I was still terrified of the investment. It was $10,000 to pay in full, or I could pay in 12 monthly instalments of $1,000.

What a commitment. I felt sick. I knew it would be pricey, but that investment terrified me. I had never spent that much on anything in my life. This was all on me. There was nobody to support this, no loans, no credit cards, it was me or nothing.

For a moment, I allowed myself to dream big. *'Imagine what's possible with that level of support'*. *'If I invest this much, imagine what I'll make back'* and *'I'll meet awesome business owners on this journey'* I thought to myself. I was just certain that I'd make the investment back, as I had done so with my previous coach.

Looking back, I realise I was truly trusting my gut, something I now pride myself on. I believe your gut can give you insights that your head or heart can't. There was something within me telling me to just go for it, so I leaned into that feeling. Right there on that call, I said yes!!!

I told her I'd love to work with her and asked if we could start in October, three weeks away to give me time to find the money for the first instalment. She politely agreed, and the countdown was on.

CHAPTER 4

I came off that call feeling insanely pumped, just before the imposter syndrome set in once again...

Who was I to spend that much on a coach? What if I wasted $12,000 and it crippled me financially? Could she really help me get to 6 figures in my business? Before I had much more time for the scary thoughts to creep in, I had sent the paperwork through and was onto my next client task.

There really was no going back now...

October came around very quickly, and I made that first instalment. It did not leave very much in my bank account after doing so, but I had committed. I trusted myself, my gut, and my coach. I knew this would be the start of something special.

A few days after I made the first payment, we had our first group session. There were several call times to choose from due to the varying time zones of other ladies in the programme, ranging from the US, UK, and Australia. I actually felt nervous getting on that first group call on the 2nd of October 2018. What if the other ladies in the programme were already having £5k or £10k months? Or more? What if they were super established? What if they belittled my business? What if they thought I was a joke and should give up now?

Once again, the "who am I" thoughts crept in...

Who am I to be in a mastermind with successful women? I'm just the horsey girl from The Cotswolds with a big dream. I even felt paranoid about my Zoom background and what I was wearing. But, with the memory that I had just paid $1,000, I thought I'd best get on the call and show up for myself.

I can't even explain how inspired I felt when I got off that first call. The vibe and energy were infectious. I had already made Facebook friends with a few girls in the group which was nice, and I actually felt like I was in a really safe space, to share comments, questions, concerns, and open up about struggles, goals, and what I was working on. Most importantly, there was space to dream big and be inspired.

I must confess, I did actually feel a little confused after the call. There was a lot of talk about mindset. What was 'mindset'?

As part of the mastermind, we had access to a lot of online pre-recorded training videos, workbooks, and PDFs which were about mindset. I thought I had signed up to work with a business coach. To me, that was systems, funnels, strategies, scaling, and marketing. Where did mindset come into it?

Another takeaway from the first call was that I was encouraged to implement a morning routine. At the time, my coach lived in South Africa but had also lived in Newcastle, Los Angeles, and Australia. To be very honest, I wondered if this 'morning routine' was a 'woo woo' thing she'd picked up on her travels around the world.

Firstly, when was I going to find time to do a morning routine? I had my horse to feed and sort, so I was busy first thing in the morning. Secondly, why did I have to? I just wanted to grow my business. I had never heard of anything like this and really didn't see the importance of it to help me hit my goal.

I remember the coach telling me there was a printable PDF to help guide a morning routine, so I printed it and said I'd give it a go.

The first time I tried it, it felt strange. I sat on my own in our kitchen, it was dark outside and there I was saying five things I was grateful for.

"How is this going to help me get to 6 figures?" I thought to myself.

I wrote out that I was grateful for my business, my husband, my animals and then got stuck. It just wasn't flowing, so I went on to the next section, Meditation.

Well, that was a step too far. *"I'm not sitting here meditating, this is The Cotswolds, not Beverly Hills,"* I told myself and others. I even told myself I was too busy to meditate and that my mind was too busy to sit quietly, even for five minutes. Looking back, they were absolute warning signs that I needed to meditate!

Nevertheless, I finished the morning routine, apart from the meditating as this was something I struggled with, and felt... Nothing. I perhaps wrongly assumed that after doing ONE, yes, just one, morning routine, I'd feel different. Perhaps I'd feel lighter, more positive, calmer, more focused, and more in control. But I felt no different.

What a total letdown.

I stuck with it for a few days before sharing my thoughts with the coach and the ladies in the mastermind. *"This isn't working for me, I don't like it and it's not making any difference,"* I exclaimed.

Upon sharing my thoughts, I was basically told to keep trying and have faith. I felt like I had been told off!! So on I went, trying it each day.

Yet still, nothing.

What I didn't realise at the time, was that this morning routine was actually offering a plethora of benefits to myself, while enhancing my mindset, something I hadn't even signed up for.

As the weeks passed, the importance of mindset work became even more apparent. I spoke with other members of the mastermind, who actually had specific mindset coaches as well as our business coach. They had recognised the shifts from starting mindset work and wanted to be able to clear what had been holding them back on an even deeper level. and they said they had done deeper subconscious work after seeing the benefits of scratching the surface through a morning routine.

The more I heard, the more I looked into it. I started to get staggered by the results of others and what I was reading.

The prevalence and importance of mindset work within the space of high achievers and the most successful business owners was vast.

Author, motivational speaker, and entrepreneur Jack Canfield puts much of his success down to mindset, meditation, and masterminding. That was a big realisation for me, as those three m's were all part of my current reality. I was in a mastermind, accidentally doing mindset work and desperately trying to meditate. Jack, an exceptionally highly regarded multi-millionaire and man of wisdom had put his success down to that magic trio.

That was a mic-drop moment for me.

"Time to sit up and listen," I thought!

Napoleon Hill is another great believer in mindset work. He is the author of *'Think and Grow Rich'* and once said, *"whatever the mind can conceive and believe, it can achieve."*

This quote is one of my all-time favourites.

The name Brendon Burchard also popped up a lot back then. He coached my coach, so feeling intrigued, I googled him too. He was the leading high-performance coach for 7 and 8-figure coaches, as well as the author and leader of the world's biggest study of high performers, which he recorded and wrote about in his book, *High Performance Habits*.

Upon my research, I found that Brendon was particularly fond of a morning routine, even producing content online about the *worst* ways to start your morning. Who knew there was a good way to start your day and a bad way?

After reading more, I realised that I and many others started the day in a way that was actually detrimental to our growth, results, and mindset. It struck a chord, yet still wasn't enough to make me truly want to change my entire morning and commit to a morning routine.

I kept reading and learning more. All of these pointers and professionals were giving me continual thoughts. "This mindset stuff must be quite important," I kept thinking. But again, I wasn't seeing the instant results I thought I'd get. It was winter at this time, so it was cold and dark outside, I really didn't want to be doing it.

There was always a little fear in the back of my mind of what others would think if they found out about my mindset work, "who am I to do mindset work, I live on a farm in The Cotswolds, it's just not something people do around here." I felt silly.

Then there was an instrumental point when it *really*, and I mean, really clicked.

CHAPTER 5

THE MOMENT WHEN IT ALL CLICKED

"Success in any area of your life is 80% mindset and only 20% strategy or skill." —Tony Robbins

As part of the mastermind I was in, we were invited to Los Angeles, California for a one-week business retreat. I booked my place and bought my plane ticket for the event that was to take place in March 2019. Once again imposter syndrome set in.

I realise now, I was really battling imposter syndrome a lot back then. It's normal when you're new in business, stepping out of your comfort zone, or accessing your next level. I've since found that anytime imposter syndrome sets in, or I feel uneasy or uncomfortable about something, it's proof that my next level is coming. I now like to call it 'new level, new devil'. But back then, I didn't recognise that. I just kept feeling like I didn't belong.

The week before the retreat, I must admit, I felt uneasy. A mix of nervousness and excitement. I had always been a confident person, so I wasn't worried about meeting new people or flying alone. It was more the fear that my business would be judged. Was I really good enough to go on this retreat? Or worthy of spending time with such epic people in a multi-million-dollar mansion?

On Sunday 24th March, I made the journey to London Heathrow to board an 11.5-hour flight to L.A. on my own. As someone who adores every aspect of plane-based travel, from airport shopping to plane food, and everything in between, I was super excited! Once I was through check-in and sat in the departures lounge, I treated myself to lunch and a glass of champagne. I got my laptop out and paid the ladies on my small team, checked in on my emails and social media, and prepared myself for one of the most exciting weeks of my life. As I sat there, laptop out, sipping the chilled glass of bubbles, I felt like a total boss. I actually felt a little smug inside and couldn't help but smile. I think it was the most grown-up and proud I'd ever felt in my life. My legs were crossed under the table and as I sat up a little taller. I held myself in the posture of a successful business woman with confidence oozing out from the inside. There was a warm, glowing feeling inside of me, not just from the bubbles, and I felt ready. No more playing small. No more letting fear or excuses hold me back. There and then, I set an intention and made a commitment to myself.

Now is the time.

The time to up-level, grow, smash some goals, and create the business I had dreamt of. This was it. The start of pure magic...

I boarded the flight and realised there was no going back. It felt like a true analogy of my entire life to that point. The cabin crew were in their positions, and we were ready for take-off, in life AND business.

Just over 14 hours later after landing at LAX, I found myself in the back of a taxi. It was pitch black outside; the sun having set over the Hollywood hills. We meandered up those prolific hills, climbing higher and higher until I heard the indicator suggesting a turning right. Where on earth were we going?! The fears that can only come from watching one too many scary movies when younger crept into play as my mind gave me all of the scary 'what ifs' about what could happen next. We had turned into a little dark road with only one streetlight at the end, and then the taxi stopped. Apparently, we were here.

With trepidation and a massive suitcase, I stepped out of the taxi and found myself faced by a huge, imposing, secretive wall and a gate of equally daunting presence.

I opened the gate and followed the steps, which meandered down through the garden, past the gorgeous big pool, and towards the beautiful house.

As I neared the house, I could hear the girls that were already there. There was a certain buzz that came from the house, one that could only be made from a group of 15+ epic, driven women. It was such a welcoming sound after a day of travelling. As I entered the house, I was met by this beautiful, big, and spacious open-plan home. By this point, I had already made friends with most of the girls from the mastermind, yet we had never actually met in person.

I could instantly feel the high vibe energy in the room. It felt really powerful, and I was so excited to be immersed in it! You could truly sense the potential, the power, and the energy of what was due to unfold.

That Sunday evening was a relaxed one of bonding over tapas, nibbles, and fizz. The ladies all seemed so lovely which really helped calm my nerves. After lots of chatting, laughing, and bonding, I went to my room, and spent a few moments journaling and celebrating things I was so grateful for before falling into a deep, exhausted sleep.

On Monday morning, I awoke fairly early, with a mixture of jet lag and excitement. I opened my bedroom window and stepped out onto the balcony. The air was fresh, with a tinge of coolness to it as the sun had yet to rise. My balcony was surrounded by trees and the hillside. The sound was magical - birds tweeting and the distant sound of the buzz fromL.A. below. I could have been anywhere in the world. And in that very moment, I was exactly where I needed to be. I took a few seconds to just breathe it in. That moment felt so magical. I felt super excited, grateful to be there, and eager with anticipation for the day ahead. I put on my maxi dress and some big earrings and went to dangle my legs in the pool, while I sat and did my morning routine. By this point, I was much more connected with my morning routine, and I actually enjoyed doing it.

Side note - *It does take at least 21 times to form a new habit, so if you're implementing something such as a morning routine, you'll need to do it consistently for at least 3 weeks for the new habit to be formed! But more on that later!*

CHAPTER 5

I was so encapsulated by the moment, I knew I wanted to document it and capture it so I could remember it forever. I snapped a photograph of my notepad and pen at the poolside, with my legs dangling in the pool. It felt like a moment worthy of influencer status. At that moment, I felt overcome with gratitude. How epic was it that I was on a high-level retreat in Los Angeles, with epic women from all across the globe. Again, I felt like a total boss stepping into my next level of brilliance. The house was silent, and as my feet paddled in the pool, I started to dream big. Questions started whizzing around my mind.

- How cool would it be to run a retreat like this?

- How much would it mean to me to be invited to speak at a retreat?

- What's next after hitting the 6-figure year?

- How can I make more of an impact in the online space for business owners?

Once I had finished my morning routine, we all sat down for breakfast. The anticipation was obvious as we eagerly awaited the first session with our coach. We had no idea what to expect from the sessions. We weren't given a timetable or guide, so I assumed the sessions would be along the lines of strategies, funnels, advertising, and marketing. I grabbed my notepad, a high-vibe pen, and with a very open mind, felt ready to get underway.

My assumptions of the coaching couldn't have been more wrong.

The *whole* week was about mindset.

We had a number of sessions from our coach as well as some from guest experts. Every single session was about mindset and completely blew my mind! We even had a powerful session aligning sex with sales, that was hosted by a coach who charged $250,000 for a 9-month coaching programme, and she actually doubled that investment straight after that session!

The breakthroughs were out of this world. Every single one of us felt a shift. We cried. We grew. We masterminded. We bonded. We hugged. We ate, we drank, and we toasted.

I remember doing some deep subconscious healing work in one of the sessions. We sat outside in the warm California sun, and I just recall having tears streaming down my face as I released the limiting beliefs, ideas, and stories I had held on to for so long. That moment will stay with me forever. It was a life-changing afternoon for me. That evening I had one of my strongest realisations about the power of mindset work, releasing negative unwanted emotions, and re-wiring limiting beliefs. The desire I have to help women achieve the same stemmed from that very emotive afternoon and the monumental shift I felt after doing that difficult inner work.

The week was everything I wanted and needed it to be, and so much more. I will truly never forget it. It was the catalyst for everything I desire, know, believe, understand, feel, and embody to this day. The week flew by and suddenly, it was time to think about heading back to the airport for that long flight home.

I felt super reflective on that flight home. I felt like a new woman. I could feel the expansion happening within me. I felt lighter, more able and capable, more driven and determined than ever before. And I recognised that I had two major realisations:

---

1. I wanted to run high-vibe, expansive retreats just like this experience.

2. Mindset work is clearly more important than I ever thought it could be.

These two realisations give SO much to my clients and audience and honestly have changed people's lives.

Yes, I had been terrified to go on that retreat. Yes, I felt total imposter syndrome many times. Yes, I cried a lot at the breakthroughs I was having and the uncomfortable memories I was working through. But it had been one of the best experiences I could have wished for. I changed and grew SO much as a person during that week. I also formed great friendships with epic women who are still my business besties.

Upon getting home, I began to think. How could I offer mindset work as part of my coaching packages and within the abundance of free content I put out into the world? Where would I even start? Could I do it?

The morning after returning home, I had my best morning routine and I felt more connected than ever before. It felt intentional and I felt more belief in what I was doing.

At last, six months after accidentally starting my mindset journey I was hooked, and it was only just beginning. I couldn't wait to learn more and support my clients on a deeper level.

As I continued to commit and connect to my morning routine, I started to see even better results. Things like setting my goal or intention for the day and then smashing it, journaling my feelings, and the ability to get through whatever the day threw at me with ease. I actually felt laser focused on my goals and my mission. Ideas from my vision board were even coming into my reality with ease and flow.

Suddenly, it was working...

CHAPTER 6

WHEN I HAD THE AWARENESS OF THE POWER AND POTENTIAL OF A MORNING ROUTINE

"Your mind doesn't know the difference between reality and what you tell it. So try telling it good things about yourself and just watch the difference unfold before your eyes."

I made my first vision board on 31st December 2018. On it, I had pictures like beaches of The Maldives, a new, fast car, as well as words and feelings I wanted to feel, such as financially abundant, wealthy, and healthy.

I looked at it daily, feeling an interchangeable mix of excitement and worry. The excitement was obvious as I gazed at the white sandy beaches, the crystal turquoise waters, and the sheer thought of going to The Maldives, somewhere I had wanted to go for so long. I would stare at that picture and just imagine, for a millisecond how it would feel to actually board a flight to go there. How it would feel to land in the seaplane, in paradise. How it would feel to walk those bright white beaches barefoot, with my love by my side and a cocktail in hand. I imagined the first dipping of my toes in the warm Indian Ocean. As I gazed longingly, I could imagine the feelings so clearly.

I could really feel the excitement around the new car as well. I'd never had a car that new, in fact, the youngest car I had up until that point was eight years old, so the thought of a brand-new car was such a treat. I'd look at the picture and imagine walking up to it and getting behind the wheel. I'd imagine how it would feel to drive it out of the showroom, to drive it along the road, to park it in a car park. I could visualise it on our drive, how it would feel to walk out to it each morning, to unlock it and get into it. I imagined how safe and lovely it would feel setting off on a long journey, knowing and trusting that it was going to get me there without any strange noises, something I was so accustomed to. I had even been on the new car configurator online to design the exact specification I'd choose. Again, I could feel those feelings so clearly!

But then the worry would strike, HOW would either of these desires ever be possible?

How on earth was I going to ever afford the Maldives? How would I afford or justify a brand-new car? What about the insurance or tax on it? It was also petrol, whereas I was used to diesel cars, could I afford to run it? The Maldives and car were massive goals, and both carried a super high value. Was I really worthy of either? I didn't know how it would happen, I just kept looking, wishing, hoping, and feeling.

CHAPTER 6

Looking back, one thing I realise that helped immensely, was my determination when I *really* wanted something. There had been many times in my past when I had wanted something and knew I just had to find a way to make it happen. My thoughts often naturally shifted from 'I can't afford this' to 'how can I afford this' and I would do whatever I could do to make it happen. That has been a consistent pattern with me and something I recognise I've picked up from my Mum, who always said *"you can have anything in life if you're willing to work for it and put your mind to it."*

What I didn't realise at the time, this is what is known as a growth mindset. Looking for ways to make things happen is one of the key traits of a growth mindset, whereas saying something can't be for me or that I can't afford it is very much a fixed mindset. Much more on that later!

Over the next few months, I continued to connect to that vision board, still not knowing how any of it would ever be possible in my reality. I was obsessed with the things on my board and then suddenly started seeing them everywhere! It seemed like the car I desired was suddenly more common, and it seemed like everybody else was also going to the Maldives. Was it a sign? Was it a coincidence? I kept believing, without knowing the how. Three months after printing my first vision board, just days before I flew to Los Angeles, I bought that brand-new car from the local Audi garage. Just a few weeks later, for my 30th birthday, my husband gave me a voucher for a one-week holiday to The Maldives.

I couldn't believe it!

I truly had no idea how either would be possible, but the universe clearly had a plan!

Seeing how quickly I was able to tick those things off my vision board also made me sit up and listen to the potential of mindset work.

With my newfound love and understanding of mindset work, and having just manifested these two epic things within 4 months, I began to wonder, what else could be possible? How much could I push this?

Could I create an even bigger and better impact? Could I help others manifest amazingness too? What about client results? I suddenly had a drive and desire to use manifestation, mindset work, and a morning routine not just for the good of myself but to really help others.

The coming weeks had me dreaming bigger than I could ever have imagined. I felt inspired, laser-focused, and ready for more. This dreaming and focus also trickled down to my clients, as I encouraged and helped them dream bigger than ever before.

I also started encouraging my clients to start a morning routine, explaining how much mine had helped me. At first, I think they thought I had lost the plot. The horsey girl from The Cotswolds was encouraging meditation and gratitude. How on earth was that going to help them hit their goals and grow their business? But as they often do, they trusted me and stuck with it, and to this day, my clients that implement a morning routine truly recognise the power of doing one, as it now gets to change their lives too.

Having seen such great results from both me and my clients with the morning routine, I wanted to take it even further. I wanted to be able to support them on an even deeper level, helping them rewire their mind, truly remove any limiting beliefs, and help them create a mindset that can support them in hitting their goals with ease. In November 2019, I qualified as a certified NLP Coach, NLP Practitioner, Hypnotherapist, and Practitioner of Time Line Therapy®.

NLP (Neuro-Linguistic Programming) can be defined as a pseudoscientific approach to communication, personal development, and psychotherapy. It was created by Richard Bandler and John Grinder. Simply put, it's about understanding how the mind works and the importance of the language we use, both internal language as well as the actual words we speak, in order to help us achieve our goals quicker, more efficiently, and effectively, and actually live a better life.

So, what does NLP break down to and how can it help us?

Neuro = Mind

Linguistic = Language you use

Programming = How your mind is wired

When we understand how our mind is wired and where our beliefs come from, we are truly able to reclaim the power over our subconscious mind, so we can use it to our advantage. It can truly be our greatest asset and ally. The truth is, as writer John Milton once said, "*your mind can either make a hell out of heaven or a heaven out of hell,*" meaning it can either have your back, cheer you on to see the greatest moments in the most difficult of situations, or it can always be holding you back, always be glass half empty, and always believe that nothing is ever good enough. I'm sure you can recognise which you'd prefer. This is the difference between doing mindset work and not.

Doing mindset work = your mind has your back, cheers you on, and is your greatest asset.

Not doing mindset work = your mind will keep you stuck, you'll always question yourself, and your mind isn't the vibey fun place to hang out.

The seven-day NLP training was super insightful, there were so many 'a-ha' moments throughout it, and moments when my mind felt blown. Understanding the impact of the language we use alone is staggering. One of the greatest, yet simplest learnings for me, was that your mind doesn't know the difference between reality and what you tell it.

Read that again.

"Your mind doesn't know the difference between reality and what you tell it."

So many of us are our own harshest critics, often putting ourselves down, or telling ourselves we can't do something. Think back to the last time you told yourself "I'm not confident, capable, worthy" or "I can't do that." We tell ourselves these stories all day every day, they run on complete autopilot and subconsciously hold us back. Yet, it doesn't have to be this way. So many people don't realise they actually have control over their thoughts and can use them to their advantage. That's what I really want to help you achieve throughout this book so that you can be free of the negative thoughts and beliefs that have potentially held you back for so long.

What happens with that negative inner chatter, is that your subconscious mind will just believe it all to be true. It won't question it, it won't challenge it, it'll just believe it to be true. That's where the saying "tell yourself something enough and you'll believe it" comes from.

So, what are the inner stories you tell yourself over and over again? It could be a story that comes up as a protection mechanism to keep you safe, or it could be a story based on something you heard when you were younger, that just gets repeated over and over again as a protection mechanism.

Your mind will believe every thought you have. It has no way to determine whether those thoughts are false information or not, so it just keeps on believing everything you tell it. The second crucial thing to understand and remember when it comes to your mind is that *what you believe is what you will achieve.*

"What you believe is what you will achieve."

Let's say that your mind doesn't know whether your thoughts are real or not, and it just believes everything it hears, and then what you believe is what you achieve. If your thoughts are negative, putting you down and making you question yourself, the result will rarely be a positive outcome. If you've had the inner story for decades that you're not confident, and your mind believes it, then what you will achieve is a lack of confidence in your life or business, which will manifest itself as ways that you stay stuck. If the inner story is that you're not good enough, your mind will believe it, then you will achieve the feeling and experience of not being good enough.

It may start as an innocent passing thought, story, or belief, but its power is so much more than that.

Based on these two pointers alone, we can start to see the power of the mind and how it can either be our greatest asset or our most destructive opponent. It can either have our back or it can hold us back. When used properly and carefully, it can lead you to greatness. When you're out of control with it, it really can be working against you and can constantly keep you from achieving what you desire and dream of.

So, what has this got to do with a morning routine?

Let's explore more.

CHAPTER 7

HOW DOES YOUR MIND FUNCTION & HOW DOES THIS RELATE TO A MORNING ROUTINE?

"Your present circumstances don't determine where you go, they determine where you start." —Dr. Lauren Fogel Mersey

By now, you're probably wondering how on earth a morning routine can make a difference in your life and business? Well, thank you for sticking around this far, because that's exactly what we're going to explore in this chapter. I will share with you the exact steps to create and make your morning routine work for you, no matter what you have going on in your life, career, and business!

First of all, let's talk about your mind and how it functions to help you understand how a morning routine can help you change your mindset.

Your mind is split into two parts - the conscious and the subconscious. The subconscious is sometimes known as the unconscious; they are exactly the same part, but some feel that calling the subconscious mind *sub*conscious implies its *sub*-par, which is very much not the case. Throughout this book and in all of my teachings, I will refer to it as the subconscious mind.

The subconscious mind takes up a staggering 95% of your total mind and is one million times more powerful than the conscious mind. This is the part we wish to change when wanting to work on and improve our mindset. That being said, both parts have very clear and important roles to play.

Conscious - This is the part of your mind that contains all thoughts, memories, feelings, and wishes that you are *aware of* at any given moment. It's very much set in the now. This is how we think about and talk about things rationally. Your aspirations and dreams come from your conscious mind. The conscious mind can easily be changed in a moment.

Subconscious - This guides our automatic movements and behaviours every day. The subconscious mind holds your beliefs, habits, memories, and emotions. It has one primary function: to keep you safe and alive. The beliefs of the subconscious mind will determine whether your aspirations from your conscious mind will come to fruition or not. Unlike the conscious mind, the subconscious mind is more stubborn, having decades of evidence to support it.

I love how Özge Longwill states the difference in an article written for Medium; *"Your subconscious mind mostly listens to the big guy, your conscious mind. Your conscious mind plants the seeds and your subconscious mind lets them germinate and grow freely. The next time you attempt to speak badly of yourself, remember this."*

When doing work to improve the mindset, it is the subconscious mind that we wish to work with, as this is the part that will actually be holding you back.

So how exactly is it holding you back?

Your current mindset and belief system are something you've been holding onto for a very long time. Your beliefs were completely set subconsciously when you were less than seven years old. As a young child, you would hear things from parents, at school, in the media, or on TV and draw conclusions about the meaning. Let's explore what that might look like.

You may have heard that *"money doesn't grow on trees."*

Which made you believe it's really hard to have money.

You may have heard that *"girls should be seen and not heard."*

Which made you believe you can't speak what's on your mind.

You may have heard *"we can't afford that."*

Which made you believe you can't have what you want in life.

You may have been told *"don't cry."*

> Which made you believe you can't show or feel your emotions.

All of these beliefs are formed without your awareness. When the human mind is less than seven years-old, it is in a sponge-like, moldable, and receptive state. This means the mind is able to absorb everything, in a super learning state. It is also a key point at which beliefs can be changed.

This is where a morning routine can actually thrive because your mind is in that exact same state in your first waking hour of every single day throughout adulthood. It's moldable, so you can change the wiring of it, and it's receptive, so it's less likely to challenge what you think.

If you're really wanting to change your beliefs, your first waking hour is the key time to do so!

Now ask yourself this - how do you spend your first hour of waking?

So many people are in the habit of reaching for their phone as soon as they wake up and checking their social media, emails, and notifications. I know, I used to. If you can truly say that it doesn't affect your mindset or how you feel in your day, then great. But for so many it really has a negative impact, myself included.

Even if you don't feel like it impacts you, there is actually research and studies to back up the negative implications. Bestselling author and the world's leading high-performance coach, Brendon Burchard states that when you start your day by checking social media, you're actually starting it from a place of comparison. He goes on to mention that scrolling is actually addictive. When you scroll, it gives your brain new information, which releases dopamine, the feel-good hormone, and transmitter. Your mind and body can actually get addicted to the release of that feel-good hormone, which is why you can find yourself excessively scrolling and suddenly losing thirty minutes or more of your precious time.

When many of us scroll through social media, it makes us feel either positive or negative. If you can scroll and feel totally inspired by what you see, then that's just amazing, and I'm so pleased for you. But if it makes you feel fed up, unworthy, like you're not good enough, or it puts you in a negative mood, it is time to recognise that and do things that actually make you feel better. We can't control what we see on social media. Even if you have a closely guarded friends list and only follow people that inspire you, you can still get triggered by something or be made to feel not good enough by someone sharing their achievements.

The same applies to your inbox. You have little to no control over what lands in there. I think it's also important to mention that your email inbox is somebody else's agenda, it's *their* to-do list and what they need from *you*. For example, let's say you've just woken up, reached over, grabbed your phone, and opened your emails, and there's one in there that isn't very nice. Maybe it's an unhappy customer or an annoyed email from your boss or co-worker. Receiving that email in that instance is going to instantly put you into a bad mood, set a negative vibe for the day, and potentially ruin your entire day.

The truth is, there is generally very little in your inbox that can't wait a couple of hours until you're in full-on work mode.

This took me a long time to master - I no longer have notifications on my phone, and I removed the email app. I remember one evening, Si and I were sitting at home having just had a lovely dinner and I saw an email pop up, at about 9:30 pm. I saw the first few sentences and I just had to read them.

It was a past client getting really irate. I was speechless and rather angry at the situation. I felt annoyed that she had come into my inbox, out of working hours, on a Friday night, been rather rude, and I allowed it to negatively impact the rest of my evening. I went to bed pissed off, didn't sleep well, and woke up in a terrible mood. Unfortunately, this was before the days of doing my morning routine, so the bad mood I woke up in stayed with me all day. I didn't realise I could actually get myself out of the bad mood and into a better one. Whereas now I know that my morning routine can snap me out of any of those funks! It also turns out that she was having a bad day, hence reaching out to me in a negative way, which she later apologised for in her email.

So now, I don't check any social media or emails until I'm ready to start my working day, which is generally at least 2-3 hours after I get up. I do what I need to do and get myself ready for work. Even though I work and run my business from home, I still think it's important to get myself 'ready for work'. I'm then in work mode and because I've prepared myself so well, I'm truly ready to face whatever the day throws at me. It's easier to handle the more difficult situations that arise in your day when you've prepared yourself properly, taken control of your thoughts, and made yourself feel good.

I was amazed to learn that choosing how you wish to feel has a positive impact on your immune system. While reading Becoming Supernatural, by Dr. Joe Dispenza, I was left speechless, which doesn't happen often, by a piece of research he shared.

Being in a feeling of contentment, love, joy, gratitude, or inspiration increases the production of immunoglobulin A (IgA), a protein marker for the strength of the immune system.

Dr. Dispenza states, *"IgA is an incredibly powerful chemical, one of the primary proteins responsible for healthy immune function and the internal defence system. It's constantly fighting a barrage of bacteria, viruses, fungi, and other organisms that invade or are already living within the body. It's so powerful that it's better than any flu shot or immune system booster you could possibly take. When it's activated, it's the primary internal defence system in the human body. When stress levels (and therefore the levels of stress hormones like cortisol) go up, this lowers levels of IgA, thereby compromising and downregulating the immune system's expression of the gene that makes this protein."*

He goes on to say that in a study at one of his workshops, he asked participants to move into an elevated emotional state such as love, joy, inspiration, or gratitude for ten minutes, three times a day. He wondered if we could elevate our emotions, could we boost our immune system?

The results were staggering; average IgA levels were up by 49.5%! The test subjects showed significant, measurable epigenetic changes without changing their external environment. They simply changed how they felt.

Mind blown.

If this isn't proof to get yourself into a positive, joyful, happy state more often I don't know what is! Imagine what you could achieve with a healthy immune system. No need for sick days or feeling under the weather, you could be functioning at a higher level more of the time.

Imagine for a second that one of those ten-minute gratitude and joy activities is part of your first hour of waking. This is a time when your mind is absorbing everything and is in a state where it can be shifted. Not only are you setting yourself up for daily success, but you're also boosting your immune system.

Task

Throughout this book, I want to give you actionable steps so you can start to shift your mindset. Today, we're starting with an awareness piece.

Ask yourself: How do you start your day? What are you doing, seeing, reading, or thinking in your first hour of the day? Do you reach for your phone? Look at social media? Open the news app? Check your messages and emails? Do your thoughts get away with you? Are you guilty of letting your thoughts spiral before you even get out of bed? Do you find yourself worrying about the same things day after day?

Allow yourself to have that awareness and then, I invite you to consider how that makes you feel. Do you feel like you're comparing yourself? Do you feel like you're not good enough? Does something upset you or make you feel negative? Do you recognise your thoughts start to spiral? Do you wake up and instantly feel anxious, worried, or fearful?

I invite you to be really honest with yourself here. The aim of this task is to bring awareness to what you do and to which habits are potentially having a negative impact on how you feel going through your day. I don't want you to start feeling guilty about how you have previously started your day. I want you to have the awareness so you can reclaim your power over your thoughts, feelings, and ultimately, your day.

Now, each morning in your first waking hour, I invite you to think of three good things going on in your life. It can be anything, the sunrise, the calm morning, the roof over your head, a good night's sleep, your warm coffee, or even your smile. The aim is to bring awareness to three good things into your morning so you can start small in the shift to a greater mind and a better outlook on life.

CHAPTER 8

HOW CAN A MORNING ROUTINE HELP YOU DEAL WITH THE DAY?

"When you start your day with gratitude, beauty shines from within."

There are so many amazing things that a morning routine can help you with, and we're going to explore the many ways it can support your personal development journey and growth, as well as your goals. There are so many ways in which you can partake, which we'll go through in this book.

Doing a morning routine isn't just about helping you think positive. It's about building up resilience, believing in yourself, and working towards a more appealing future. It's about preparing yourself for whatever the day may throw at you. It's about getting yourself into a peak state, ready to thrive. And getting yourself so focused on your day, intention, and work that nothing can knock you off kilter. Because life happens and sometimes things can really challenge us. Starting your day the right way can really help give *you* an advantage.

There have been a number of times, both personally and professionally, when I've been so grateful for my morning routine and the strong mindset it has helped me develop.

For the first five years of my business, I believed in order to make more money, I had to work more hours, hustle, and work as hard as I possibly could.

From 2017 to 2020, my hustle mentality was the worst. I would burnout several times every year, generally every three months. I'd recognise the signs of burnout when I'd sit down at my laptop to start work in the morning and my mind wouldn't even be able to construct a reply to a client's email. It's like my brain literally wouldn't function. I began to recognise that I was not good for anything in that state and would have to clear my diary. On many occasions that burnout would last a whole week and I would lay on the sofa watching crappy daytime TV. I'd constantly feel angry at myself. I was letting my clients down time and time again, as well as letting myself down, and being fairly useless to the world.

The guilt would soon creep in. How was I continually letting my paying clients down? This wasn't very professional. Would word get around that I was letting people down and cancelling their sessions last minute?

This was a destructive cycle I knew I had to stop.

The last time I burnt out was the worst. It was a Friday morning in September 2020, and I was truly exhausted. Due to the lockdowns of the pandemic, I genuinely hadn't stopped since we had our last holiday in January of that year. Work was thriving, my coaching programmes were constantly sold out, and I was making decent money. Yet, there was absolutely no balance, no rest, no lunch breaks, and I was even working weekends. My body was exhausted. My mind was exhausted. It was a full-on week, but it didn't feel much different from any other. I was just totally wiped out. Perhaps my energy was naturally lower, or perhaps I wasn't eating or sleeping as well. I remember telling myself that the very next day would truly be an introvert day. I didn't want to do anything or see anyone.

I got up on that Saturday morning and couldn't move my left shoulder and arm, it felt totally locked. I wondered if I had slept on it funny. Nevertheless, I struggled out of bed and managed to get ready so I could feed and muck out my horse. It was all a real struggle, I couldn't do the simplest of tasks with one working arm and one locked shoulder. I rang my husband and asked him to come and help.

I was in such pain. Upon getting back in the house, I put a strappy top and my pyjama bottoms on, took some painkillers, and told Si I was going to fill a hot water bottle before retreating to the sofa to rest.

As I was filling the hot water bottle with boiling water from the kettle, it somehow exploded and in a split second, I was covered in boiling water. The boiling water straight out of the kettle covered my left shoulder and chest.

CHAPTER 8

At first, I was in shock. Si shouted "oh my gosh" with sheer worry. For a moment, I thought I was OK. The adrenalin helped me walk slowly from the kitchen into the living room, I sat down, and then it hit me. The pain was unreal, I felt like I was going to pass out - I've truly never felt anything like it in my entire life. I struggled to breathe and for a moment I just sat on the sofa, bent over, unable to do or say anything, while the pain coursed through my entire body. I then struggled my way back into the kitchen and told Si to call an ambulance immediately. Even saying those words was difficult with the pain.

As Si was speaking to the emergency services, I slouched myself over the kitchen sink, tears running down my face. I couldn't get away from the pain. While it was the shoulder and chest area that was in agony, my whole body felt horrendous. I remember running the cold tap and just holding my hand under it, occasionally splashing it onto my face and body to try and cool myself down. I couldn't even speak. It was all a total blur.

When the paramedics got there, they asked me how I did it. I tried to explain, but due to the unbearable pain I was in, my mind just wouldn't work properly. I was given gas and air, as well as very strong painkillers, and taken to A&E in the ambulance. The ambulance staff were so lovely, I had one of them sit in the back with me and as the drugs started to kick in, I remember bantering with him. It made the whole situation much more bearable. There were short seconds where I forgot what was happening as I laughed with the wonderful paramedic. I remember feeling very grateful at that moment for such lovely support. We arrived at the hospital and the paramedics sat me in a wheelchair and pushed me into A&E.

I sat there by myself, in agony, feeling very alone. Si wasn't allowed to come with me in the ambulance or to the hospital due to the pandemic. As I sat there waiting patiently, my thoughts spiralled. I knew there and then that this was my body's way of enforcing rest. I had been shattered for days, running on empty, and using adrenalin to keep me going. My body and the Universe knew I had to stop, hence this accident, forcing me to stop. Well, I certainly had to stop now. The time in the hospital that day was horrid. I felt so alone, and I was in so much pain. I just wanted to blame myself. The procedure to deal with the burnt skin was so unpleasant, it made me feel so sick. I remember talking to the doctor about food and beach holidays, anything to keep my mind busy.

Later that afternoon, I was told I could go home but had to return the next day. Over the coming two weeks, I went to the hospital seven times. I cleared my diary, knowing I had to rest. Just two and a half weeks after the accident, I was due to host my very first in-person luxury retreat. I had ten epic ladies travelling from all over the country. This event had been due to take place in March, six months prior but had to be postponed due to the lockdown. I couldn't push it back again.

I knew how much this event would mean for the ladies, and how much they were looking forward to it. I knew my healing thoughts had to be positive, I had to be focused, and I had to rest.

So, my morning routine for those few weeks was around gratitude that the burn wasn't worse. I was grateful for my small team that ran the company when I couldn't, and my husband for sorting my horse out for me. I was grateful for my amazing clients giving me the time

I needed to rest and recover. I was also grateful for the NHS and painkillers that managed the pain! Sometimes it really is the small things that we have to be grateful for.

I journaled on the experience and made a promise to myself to never allow myself to burn out again. I'm making these final edits to this book in December 2022 and I'm so proud to say I haven't burnt out since that fateful time over two years ago.

I share that story to hopefully help you understand the importance of your rest, self-care, your body, and your mental health. Success doesn't mean anything if you can't enjoy it or if it comes to the detriment of YOU.

I do look back on that time with a positive learning. My mindset got me through. The mindset I have grown and strengthened through a consistent morning routine. Each morning during those few weeks, I committed to that time for me. I was as consistent as I had ever been, and I know it got me through. It really helped me focus on what I wanted, to heal and recover quickly rather than subconsciously focusing on what I didn't want, scarring, a skin graft, prolonged pain, and more hospital trips.

My mindset and morning routine supported my healing and two and a half weeks later, I made it to that amazing retreat venue, ready for a life-changing few days with my clients.

There have been countless other occasions whereby the morning routine has helped me stay focused, positive, and better able to deal with tricky situations and challenging times.

It really does help guide your focus and support you in starting your day the right way. It helps you find things to be thankful for, support your goals, and stay mentally strong, so you too can deal with whatever gets thrown your way.

So how can you start to craft yours?

Let's dive straight in!

PART TWO

CHAPTER 9

GRATITUDE

*O*ne thing I feel we can all get behind and feel good about is gratitude.

I truly feel that gratitude, or the science of being grateful, is one of the most underused tools we have within us to help us change our internal state and create the life of our dreams.

Stay with me here... It's not the fluffy BS you may think it is!

When you were younger, you were probably told 'to always be thankful for what you have.' In essence, this is being grateful. But as you grew up and formed into the adult you are today, you may have lost sight of gratitude.

In the book, *Becoming Supernatural,* by Dr. Joe Dispenza, he explains gratitude superbly well. He states *"gratitude is a powerful emotion to use for manifesting because normally we feel gratitude after we receive something. So the emotional signature of gratitude means it has already happened. When you are thankful or feel appreciation, you are in the ultimate state to receive your desire or wish. When you embrace gratitude, the subconscious mind will begin to believe it is in the future reality, in the present moment."*

There is a saying within the law of attraction space that states 'you can only have what you already are.' The key is to be grateful for what you have now *and* desire more. If you can only have what you already are, and you currently feel like you don't have enough money, freedom, and success) then that's all you're going to get more of. Whereas if you can be grateful for what you have now, even if you desire more, and grateful knowing you do desire more, you're much more likely to be able to attract what you desire.

Morning gratitude's are a really great way to help you focus on not only how you want your day to go, but your month, quarter, year, and life.

When you connect to the feelings and emotions of gratitude for what you have and what you desire, even if it hasn't yet happened, you'll be teaching your mind and body about what your future will *feel* like.

Too many of us live in the past, stuck on what went wrong yesterday rather than looking to what we're going to do or wish to achieve today.

Gratitude also works exceptionally well as you can't feel negative, unwanted feelings when you're in a true state of being grateful. The universal law of gratitude, which was so beautifully explained in the book *The Magic* by Rhonda Byrne, states that **"gratitude creates even more abundance; you can only have what you already are."**

I think this is a really impactful sentence - if you can only have what you already are, then we know we can reclaim the power over our current situation and our desires. This is where a lot of people get stuck. They let life happen to them and let their negative thoughts and limiting beliefs control them. They put their happiness, joy, or success up on a pedestal and claim they'll be happy *when* they hit the goal or get the thing. Putting your future happiness on an external event will never create the result you desire today. You'll constantly be chasing that feeling. The disconnect happens because you'll constantly move the goalpost. You'll hit that goal or get that thing and realise it can't sustain the happiness you desire. So, you'll end up creating the next pedestal for your happiness.

Now, I'm not saying it's a bad thing to desire or want more. I'm the biggest advocate for constantly wanting to upgrade my entire life, wardrobe, experience, and business. I do so knowing I'm already happy, successful, and abundant in all areas. Things don't make me happy. I'm happy and grateful for what I have, and I get to desire more. This is a key shift that needs to occur.

I will say, even when I was broke, I was still able to be grateful for what I had. The gratitude list may shift from time to time based on where you're at in life, career, or business and that's OK.

The beauty of gratitude is that it works on any level - you can be grateful for the smallest of things in your day, such as a delicious coffee, the warmth of your heating, or the roof over your head. And you can find gratitude in the bigger things, such as a holiday, a new car, your company, or your career. The aim is to truly focus on what you **do** have in your life, rather than what you **don't** have. Another teaching behind the law of attraction is that what you focus on expands, which is where gratitude can help you thrive.

If you're focusing on the lack of money, clients, things, or lack of a promotion, then that is where your energy will go, towards lack. Gratitude can help you shift that paradigm and bring your focus to what you have and what you desire, and ensure you're doing so from the right energy, vibe, and frame of mind.

I actually love to start each day with a gratitude rampage, where for a full minute I just list out all of the things I'm grateful for. It looks something like this.

I am grateful for my dog. I am grateful for my coffee machine.

I am grateful to live where we do. I am grateful for the countryside.

I am grateful for my husband. I am grateful for my clients.

I am grateful for my companies.

I feel so pumped and positive after!! I also do it any time that I need to shift myself back into a positive state. As I've stated several times already, you can do the best morning routine in the world but sometimes, something can just happen that knocks your mindset, inner joy, and focus off. Having the tools and ability to get yourself back into a high vibe "I've got this" state when something less than ideal happens is a really fantastic quality to possess. You really can be in control of your mind, your thoughts, your feelings, and your emotions, but it has to start with awareness, and then we can introduce the tools to help you shift your state.

It's also really useful because there will be times when you will find yourself around someone who is naturally negative. One thing I learnt while doing my NLP qualification, which I remind myself of daily.

"Everyone is doing the best they can with the mindset and skills that they have available."

That is certainly a side-effect of doing mindset work! You get more positive, more focused, you start to feel better, you're able to cope with any situation, and you can see the good in anything and everything. It makes you realise that more people need to work on their own mindset.

This sixty-second rampage can really get you into an epic mood. As you say the things you're grateful for, really feel the joy and gratitude in your chest and in your heart. And if you can go for more than one minute, please do! You'll feel sensational!

While being grateful has many surface benefits, such as helping you feel more positive, enjoy more experiences, improve your health, deal with challenges, and enhance your relationships, it can also change how you see the world.

Every single second, the subconscious part of your mind takes in millions of pieces of information - a staggering amount to even comprehend let alone process. This is obviously way too much for you or your mind to deal with, so there is an internal filtering system that takes just seven pieces, + or - two pieces, every second. That in itself is a staggering feat. Yet how it chooses which seven pieces to give you is even more staggering. It chooses based on your mood, energy, and focus in that very second. It gives you more of what you're thinking about and feeling, as that's what it thinks you want and need.

If you are thinking fed-up, negative, angry thoughts, the filtering system will find seven things every second, out of a possible million+, that are in line with that. So things that will make you feel even more fed up, negative and angry, as that's what it thinks you want. This is how you can easily get stuck in a negative rut. Our minds are actually controlling more of how our day pans out than we think or realise.

The really great news is that you can get stuck in a positivity rut, which is where I now spend most of my life. But trust me, it hasn't always been that way! If you are able to start your day from a really positive, grateful place, then you're much more likely to be able to maintain that throughout your day.

Think negatives all the time — you'll get even more of them. Think of the things you're grateful for and all of the good stuff in life — you'll get even more of that!

This isn't 'woo woo'... This is actual science. You can't argue with science!

In *Becoming Supernatural*, author Dr. Joe Dispenza explains further how detrimental being stuck in a negative rut can be. He states that your brain monitors your chemical state and the moment you feel angry, it's going to think more corresponding thoughts equal to how you feel. He uses the example of not enjoying your job, those thoughts might be along the lines of "my boss is a jerk, I should quit my job, my coworker stole my idea and I'm right and everyone else is wrong." This circuit of beliefs continually goes round and round in your head, which reaffirms your identity, in this case, being angry, in your forebrain. At this point, the limbic brain, the part responsible for emotions and memory, creates more neuropeptides that signal the same hormones from your third energy centre, in your solar plexus. This results in you feeling more agitated and angrier. And the vicious circle continues.

Dr. Dispenza highlights that this cycle of anger and frustration can go on for decades - much like being stuck in a negative rut can - by which point the brain has been hardwired into the pattern of anger. This hardwiring repeatedly conditions the body emotionally to the past. This stored energy produces a corresponding biological effect which can then manifest as issues and disease within the body, such as adrenal fatigue, digestive problems, kidney issues, or a weakened immune system, not to mention other psychological effects like a short temper, impatience, frustration, or intolerance. Over the years, you keep producing the same thoughts that keep signalling the same feelings and you continue hardwiring your brain in this very finite pattern, and as Dr. Dispenza puts it so clearly, you keep reconditioning the body and become the mind of anger.

You might think this is an extreme case. What I have witnessed with many clients that I have done deep subconscious mindset work with, is their issues started as small concerns or niggles, before developing into something much deeper. Using Dr. Dispenza's example of disliking your job, you might start by occasionally being annoyed at your boss or colleagues, as more things start to get to you and make you feel down you end up hating and resenting your work and potentially, your life. If you consider how much of your life you spend at work, on average, one-third of your life is spent working, it's easy to see how unhappiness in the workplace can easily manifest into worse things. If you're driving to work every day feeling sad about going, and something at work triggers you, then you stir about how you feel on the way home, that's a lot of time and energy spent in a negative mindset.

Now I know we have to work. That is part of life. So how can we either not let it get to us, or better yet change that situation?

I think it's important that you're able to find gratitude in your every day, not just in exciting or exceptional conditions. It's also vital that you're able to find the good in a situation or scenario when things go wrong. This really does take time and practice but is such an incredibly powerful tool to have. This alone will change your life if you're willing to stick to it.

In March 2020, the pandemic hit here in the U.K. During that first week of lockdown, I lost PR and marketing clients every single day. At that point, my company had two branches - the coaching side, and the PR and marketing side. Shortly before that lockdown hit, I also had to make the decision to postpone my first luxury up-level retreat. I was gutted. So much hard work, planning, and effort had gone into the retreat. I know how excited the guests were for the high-vibe transformation.

I was just so overcome with sadness that week. I kept doing my morning routine but actually felt like I was just doing it as a box-ticking exercise. That week, I also started watching the news, having not watched it for many years before that. As the week went on, I just felt more and more crushed. The clients kept leaving as fear transcended the world. It felt like I was watching a crappy movie of my life. I felt lost.

One morning, while mucking my horse out, I burst into tears. I was just devastated. Si came over and asked if I was OK and gave me a big hug. "What if this is the end of my business?" I wept into his shoulder. It felt so good to let the emotion out, as it always does. I just cried and cried. My business is my baby - I adore it so much and the fear-based thought that it could be taken away from me was unbearably sad. After a few minutes, I got myself together and carried on tending to my horse.

I remember that day vividly. It was particularly sunny and warm, I didn't have any coaching or client calls booked in, so I decided to take the day off and grabbed Kiwi, my little Jack Russell, and went off to walk in the quiet woods in the next-door village. I always find woods extremely calming, especially when it's sunny and the bright rays dance through the treetops.

In this particularly wooded area, there is a beautiful, peaceful stream running through the bottom, meandering through the trees. I spent some much-needed alone time in those woods. I had no phone signal which was total bliss, and I just walked and walked. Kiwi went in the stream and loved it! She had such a great time. The sun continued to pour through the tall trees, glistening on the ground. It was noticeably warm for this time of the year, and it felt so good to be out in nature, miles from anywhere or anyone and far away from what was happening in the world. There was a part of the woods where a footpath went out across a field, so I went out to lay on the grass with Kiwi.

I took some big, slow, and deep breaths in, and felt flooded with gratitude. The world looked so beautiful. It felt so peaceful and so calm. As the warm sun hit my face, I made a choice there and then. I was going to look for the good in this strange, unknown situation. I lay there, gazing up at the sky, Kiwi mincing around next to me, and did a gratitude prayer to the universe. I was grateful for the sunshine, the smell of spring in the air, the birds tweeting, this beautiful space, the blue skies, the warmth of the sun on my face, being in a T-shirt, and having the time and space in my calendar to do this. That moment instantly perked me up.

Kiwi and I carried on exploring for a little while longer before deciding to head back. I felt like a different person when I got back to our house, almost like someone had pressed the reset button. It felt wonderful, for a few hours.

Later that afternoon I made the mistake of spending too much time scrolling social media and then watching the news. That good mood I had created for myself was gone in an instant. Once again, I felt sad and like my world was crashing down. I had given my power away again. That was the moment I realised the negative impact that watching the news and scrolling social media had on me when I'm in a fragile state. That was the point I decided to stop watching it for good. The next day, another sunny one, was news free and started with a focused and intentional morning routine. I really was grateful for my life, my business, my clients, my team, and what I had created. I was able to feel joy, despite the madness going on in the world.

I truly believe that gratitude, and just finding really basic, simple things to be grateful for, helped me get through that tough time. Plus, as the law of attraction states, and now understanding how the filter system in your mind works, what you focus on expands. **What you focus on expands.**

I'd love to invite you to consider, what are you actually focusing on in your daily life. Are you focusing on opportunities, things that go well for you, things you're proud of, grateful for, and things that you get to do? Or are you focusing on how everyone else but you seem to have a great life, how there's never enough, or how everything is against you? That focus has much more of an impact than you will ever realise, so it's time to take action, have some kindness for yourself for what you've created so far, and know you're truly able to create magic!

It does require some work to get you to the point where you're able to see good in every situation, but I promise you it is so worth it. When your subconscious mind is on your side and the filtering system is working for you, your life can truly flourish. You really will find it much easier to stay in a place of pure life enjoyment.

So, how do you get started?

Task

1. Write out ten things you're grateful for right now. Really try and *feel* how grateful you are for each of those things. Think about your friends, health, family, home, animals, ability to read, etc. It can be super basic. The key is to find joy in every day.

2. Commit to saying or writing out ten things you're grateful for each morning for the next week - make sure it is in your first hour of waking.

3. If you live with someone, could you ask them ten things they're grateful for as well?

4. Next time something goes wrong, ask yourself, what am I grateful for in this situation? Perhaps it's a positive learning, an opportunity, or a reminder.

CHAPTER 10

AFFIRMATIONS

By now I hope you're understanding a little more about how the brain works and you're hopefully starting to understand the importance of thinking positively, shifting your focus, and trying to be in control of your thoughts. Having a strong mindset isn't just about thinking positively. When you work on your mindset, your view of the world really does shift into a more positive state. From this state of mind, you can be, do, have, and create so much more. So, let's dive into affirmations.

We've touched on the understanding that the mind doesn't know the difference between reality and what we tell it. Our mind is a superpower and must not be underestimated.

As a noun, an affirmation is 'the action or process of affirming something' meaning, you confirm or validate something. However, an affirmation within positive psychology refers to the act and practice of positive thinking and empowering self-talk. Within this context, an affirmation is a positive, powerful, "I am" statement. The thing with affirmations is that your mind believes every single thing and story that you tell it. That's where the saying 'tell yourself something enough and you might just believe it' comes from. It really is one of your mind's most powerful qualities. So how can you use that to your advantage?

I truly believe that affirmations are one of the most powerful parts of the morning routine. They are something I've been practising consistently since October 2018 - through the good times and the bad. They've helped me launch new offerings and sell out my offers just using Instagram stories, and they've helped me continually smash my goals and grow my companies. If I'm ever short on time, affirmations are non-negotiable for me.

Every single day you have approximately 70,000 thoughts, many of which are negative or repetitive. This is how your mind functions. A large proportion of those thoughts will be inner thoughts and an inner story, the story you're telling yourself as you go about your day. The majority of these happen completely subconsciously - meaning that generally, you have absolutely no idea they're happening. They're just mumbling along in the background as you go about your day. You might believe they're just thoughts that are happening to you, but they are forming part of your future truth. That inner story really does play an important part when it comes to your overall mindset. Taking control of your thoughts is a really important practice and something we'll discuss later in the book.

There are SO many negative limiting thoughts and ideas that people have, but in my time as a coach, some of the most popular that have come up for people are:

"I'm not good enough"

"I'm not worthy"

"I'm not confident"

"I can't do that"

"It's OK for them but not for me"

"I'm rubbish with money"

It's baffling how many women battle these thoughts, again, completely subconsciously, on a daily basis. I had been telling myself for years and years, I wasn't good with money and that it was really hard to earn, make and keep the money. Just imagine how many times I was affirming that to myself. At times, my experience of life and business totally backed that up. There were times when I couldn't even afford food, fuel, or tampons. I recall having to ask my Mum to borrow money for fuel, sometimes asking for just £10, putting £8 of fuel in my car, and using the rest to get tampons.

When I was living that truth, I was stuck in a cycle. I was constantly telling myself "I'm broke, I'm not good with money, and making money is really hard", so my physical reality backed that up with the lack of money in my bank account. It took years before I realised how damaging that inner story I'd been telling myself was. This negative relationship I had with money started when I was 18 years old and continued through University. I'd easily blow my student loans within a week or two of them landing in my account.

This bad relationship with money nearly ruined my business in April 2017. I was owed a lot of money and didn't have a single penny to fall back on. It was in July 2019 that I knew something really had to change. I had been doing mindset work for 10 months and was still in a poor financial position, living month to month and not having any control over my money and spending. Crucially, I was still telling myself that negative inner story. I just kept telling myself I was so bad with money, that it was hard to come by, that I'd always be in this situation. I realised that I had been telling myself and living out that story for well over a decade. I knew I had some serious work to do.

The recognition of your thoughts, your inner story, and your beliefs is crucial for your progress. What is also crucial is that upon recognising them, you immediately ask yourself if that thought is serving you well. Is it helping you get to where you want to be in life? Is it helping you be the business owner, person, parent, or partner that you truly want to be? Is it going to help you evolve and be the best human possible? Really ask yourself those questions and when you recognise that those thoughts aren't serving you, then you can stop the thought in its path and think a better thought.

At that point, I realised that living in a scarcity mentality with a lack mindset wasn't going to change anything. As I said, I had been doing my morning routine for some time, but perhaps hadn't truly, consistently connected to it.

I made the commitment there and then to connect to it.

The next morning, while doing my affirmations, I tried for a moment to imagine what it would feel like to be financially abundant, to be wealthy. I had been surrounded by many wealthy people before - whilst having horses, in the pubs and restaurants we went to, the area we lived in, and the University I attended. All were synonymous with wealthy people. I had been to their houses, swam in their swimming pools, seen their well-stocked wine cellars, and been in their cars. I could imagine living in their houses, one day, far away in the future! So I began to ask myself:

- How exactly would it feel to not have to worry about money?

- How would I feel each day?

- How would I act each day?

- What would my emotions be around money each day?

- How lovely would it be to just have spare money in the bank? What would that feel like?

- How would it feel to have more than enough?

I connected to those thoughts every single day. That day was a real turning point for me. That was the point I knew I couldn't go back. And pretty much every single day since then, my affirmations have been in line with the wealthier version of myself - not just wealthy in a financial sense but in terms of happiness and health for myself and others. My affirmations include:

"I am a wealthy woman"

"I am financially abundant"

"I am rich and prosperous"

"Money flows to me quickly, easily, and consistently"

"I am so open and ready to receive financial abundance"

Depending on what's going on in my business, I do often add some other affirmations that are in line with what I'm working on, such as if I'm launching a new programme or promoting something, my affirmations might look like this:

"I am a fantastic coach"

"I am so grateful and excited to put this epic programme out to the world"

"I am excited for women across the globe to have access to this programme"

"I am excited for the epic transformations this programme provides"

"I am grateful to the universe for letting me share these learnings"

"I am excited to bring this programme to the world"

Affirmations work particularly well in the morning as part of a morning routine because they help you start your day from a place of positivity and set you up exceptionally well. You've also got to remember that the thoughts you have in that first hour will have a big impact on how your day goes. If you recall from earlier in the book, in the first hour of waking, your mind is in a highly influenceable state where you truly are able to rewire the mind and belief system.

Incorporating affirmations into your morning each day will help you change the way you think, feel, and believe in yourself. It does of course take consistency but if you are committed to it, anything is possible!

So, how can your inner talk become a little bit more supportive and constructive?

Firstly, I'd like you to start recognising the thoughts you have. What does your inner dialogue say? What stories have you been telling yourself for years? Once you have that clarity, you can ask yourself what you actually want from your life, career, or business.

Next up, what thoughts and the inner story will support that? As an example:

Inner story: I'm not good enough, I'm not confident, and success isn't for people like me.

Your desire: Financial freedom, success, thriving business.

New story: I am capable, I am good enough for what I desire, and I am becoming confident.

You can basically flip your inner story so that it aligns with what you desire. You get to rewrite your story. You get to rewrite your future and you get to rewrite your destiny.

What will likely happen when you start using affirmations is that your mind will want to disprove them. You may be able to say, write or feel for a few days that you're becoming confident and you are good enough. But your powerful subconscious mind can and will try to overrule this new way of thinking. Your mind has decades of evidence and inner stories stashed away. You've got to constantly be able to bring your thoughts and inner story back to where you're wanting to go, the present and future, not where you've been in the past. Your mind will want to stay stuck in the past, playing the same stories on repeat.

I encourage you to take control of your mind, so you can keep bringing yourself, your thoughts, and your story back to what you desire.

There is an amazing NLP technique that you can use to truly take control of your mind called the Pattern Interrupt. This technique is absolute gold and so underrated. It can literally help you take control of your mind once and for all.

Any time you recognise a negative thought, story, or belief that doesn't serve and support where you're going, you can do this exercise.

First step: Recognise that a negative story, thought, or belief doesn't support you and won't help you create what you desire.

Second step: Say 'cancel, cancel, cancel', either out loud or in your mind.

Third step: Think a positive thought, say an affirmation, or align with a feeling that feels really good to you and will support you in getting what you desire.

As an example:

Thought: "I'm never going to get what I want."

Action: "Cancel, cancel, cancel. I'm excited to create my dream life."

If your mind goes into spiralling negative thoughts after saying "I'm excited to create my dream life" such as "but when", "but how" and "what if it doesn't happen" then just cancel, cancel, cancel again. Because you truly can have control over every thought.

READ THAT AGAIN!

You have control over every thought. This is something so many people don't realise - they assume their thoughts just happen to them and they let the negativity, limiting thoughts, and self-doubt get away with them, taking over their minds. They assume their mind goes off on tangents, coming up with silly scenarios, and 'what if' situations that they can't control. The good news is, every single one of us absolutely can! And here's how you can do it for yourself every single day.

Task

1. Firstly, recognise each negative thought.

2. Any time a thought comes into your mind and you're not sure if it's a good one or not, ask yourself "is this thought serving me well? Is it helping me be who I want to be? Is it helping me work towards my goals and the better life I desire?"

3. When you recognise the thought isn't helping you, stop it in its path! To do this, simply say "cancel, cancel, cancel". You can either say it out loud or in your head. This action is like cutting a piece of

string - if the string were the thought that was about to hard-wire into your mind, then cutting the string acts as the cutting off of that thought, meaning it can't hard-wire in and it's now been stopped in its path.

4. Now is your time to shine! As soon as you have said "cancel, cancel, cancel" you need to immediately replace that thought with a positive affirmation. You will find that the negative thoughts you have each day are probably very similar and often along a similar path. When you start to recognise what these are you can flip them into a positive - what is the opposite of that thought? I've put some examples in the table below.

5. Do this daily and as many times as you need to. You'll soon get bored having to repeat your three chosen words and your mind will get bored with thinking negative thoughts. Before long, positivity and upbeat affirmations will be your normality.

Negative, unwanted thought	Positive alternative
"I can't do this - it's OK for them because they're further along, had more help, or have more money"	"I can do anything and everything I put my mind to. There is no limit within me other than my mind!"
"I'm so annoyed at this situation right now, if only it were better"	"I'm in exactly the right place in my life right now and everything is working out for the best"
"Who am I to have this successful launch, life, car, or house?"	"Who am I not to, anything is possible for me"

So how can affirmations really enhance your mindset?

Success in any area of your life is 80% mindset and only 20% strategy or skill. This is true within business, your home life, and even within the sporting world. The great Muhammed Ali was known to say *"it's the repetition of affirmations that leads to belief. And once that belief becomes a deep connection, things begin to happen."*

Similarly, many sports psychologists believe in the power of positive thinking and actively removing and replacing limiting beliefs and pessimistic beliefs with positive statements and actions.

As with anything to do with your mindset, change takes time and consistency, and using affirmations is no exception.

Back in July 2019, I was totally lost. I had my first £10k+ month in the May of that year, I thought I was on a roll, and then BAM. Enquiries dried up, sales dried up, and I didn't have any new clients coming in, yet the bills continued to rise. I remember mentioning this to my coach at the time. She asked if I was still doing my morning routine, and I said I wasn't, as I couldn't connect to it, and it felt like I was just doing it as a box-ticking exercise. She encouraged me to give it a go, so the next morning, I did.

My affirmations were along the lines of "I am financially abundant," "I have everything within me to get through tough times," and "I am a fantastic money manager." It felt like I was lying to myself. I remembered that the most important thing with affirmations was to truly feel it within you. So I tried to connect with how it would feel to be financially abundant. It wasn't easy because it was so far from my reality.

What would that mean? Would it mean I never worried about money again? Would it mean there was always money in my account? I tried my hardest to connect to the feelings; I'll admit it was hard. Being in control of my mind and thoughts was hard when I had £7k worth of bills and invoices to pay and not that much money coming in, and no buffer amount or savings to play with. I think that is the hardest part - when you feel like you're drowning and you can't stop thinking about something, yet the focus of your routine or mindset work is supposed to be on the opposite of your current situation. It's really difficult! I get that.

Now that I have a better understanding of the Law of Attraction, I can see how I really was working against it. All I was focusing on was the lack of money coming in and the huge amount of bills and invoices that needed to be paid. I would say it consumed me for a whole month. It really is true that what you focus on expands, so if you find yourself in a similar situation, it is important to focus on the abundance and things coming IN, not everything that's going out! For this reason, I designed a prosperity tracker, a free downloadable PDF that you can print at the start of each month to track all that is coming in. I now track everything coming in - cash, refunds, payments, sales, vouchers I get, if there's money off of something I was going to buy anyway, if I'm given or gifted money, interest on savings accounts, if someone pays me back some money they borrowed, literally everything. Even if I found a penny on the floor, I'd pick it up and pop it in the tracker. It is all about feeling abundant and remembering, what you focus on expands! Big or small, we track it all! You can get your free printable at www.tarabest.com/book.

Another beautiful thing about affirmations is that when you say or write them AND truly feel them, you're getting into the vibration of what you desire within your body. Everything in the Universe is just energy, and as a living being you are vibrating at a frequency all the time, attracting, and bringing things into your existence. The easiest way I can describe the vibration of energy is by comparing you to a magnet. Stick with me here!

A magnet is always working - it always has a charge. All magnets have north and south poles, with opposite ends being attracted to each other. From a Law of Attraction perspective, what you attract into your life is based upon the thoughts and feelings you live on a daily basis. You will attract or become a match for, whatever energy your thoughts and feelings are vibrating at. You attract what your thoughts and feelings are.

When you get yourself into a state of feeling what you desire and are able to get yourself into the vibration as if it's already yours, then you're much more likely to attract it. Money is also just energy and it responds to your energy. If your energy, vibration, thoughts, and feelings are around scarcity, need, greed, or lack then that's all you're going to attract. If you can get into, and stay in, a state of positivity, abundance, and knowing more is on its way to you then you'll be in the right vibration to receive. Money queen and self-made multi-millionaire Amanda Frances explains the energy and vibration of money insanely well through her online content and book, *Rich As F*ck: More Money Than You Know What To Do With*. I highly recommend this book if you're wanting to improve your money mindset and understand the energy of money and having more than enough.

Committing and connecting to affirmations in a future state of how you wish to be, live, and show up really does take practice, but do stick with it. It really will help your focus, direction, and levels of self-belief as you work towards what you desire.

So, how can you create the best affirmations for yourself?

Task

1. The best way to create affirmations that will work superbly for you is to take note of the negative thoughts that run through your mind every day. Make a note of them if you can, then ask yourself "is this thought serving me?" "Do I want this thought?" "Will this thought get me from where I am to where I want to go?"

2. Next, write the positive alternative to the points you made on your list, and see how you can re-frame each point.

3. Lastly, how exactly do you wish to feel? If you could wave a magic wand, or add a sprinkling of stardust, how would you truly be, feel, and live? Dream big on this one! Then write out the list of statements as if they're already true. I've put some examples below for you.

"I am confident."

"I truly believe in myself and my abilities."

"Nothing holds me back."

"I am easily able to xxx."

"I am a fantastic money manager."

"Money flows to me easily, consistently, and from multiple sources."

CHAPTER 11

JOURNALING

Journaling is one of those things that you might have heard people talk about, but don't really know what it is. I was one of those people! I had no idea what journaling was, literally not a clue. I now adore it, it's another non-negotiable part of my daily morning routine and mindset work. It has SO many benefits and ways that it can help you.

It's a tool I've found particularly useful and one that I use in a number of situations, both as part of my daily morning routine and when I need it throughout the day.

It is basically just free writing - getting your thoughts, desires, wishes, and feelings out onto paper. It can be great for problem-solving, acting as a brain dump when you have a lot on your plate, or when you need to connect to something such as a goal or a new way of living, feeling, and being. There is no correct or incorrect way to do it - you can write it in the first or third person, in the current, future, or past tense and you can be as elaborate as you wish.

Personally, I find it works best when I use a pen and paper rather than my phone or laptop, but again, it's what works best for you.

Let's look at some of the different ways journaling can support you and how it has supported me in the past.

When I want to get into the feelings of something

How do you wish to feel? Do you wish to feel flat, negative, worried, or anxious? Or do you wish to feel joyful, abundant, positive, and high vibe? Journaling is a great tool to help you get into the desired feelings. You can literally grab a piece of paper or your notepad and start to write it out as if it's already happened. Challenge yourself to write a whole page about the feeling you desire, how great it feels, how unstoppable you feel, how life gets to be good, how everything is working out for you, and how you're so grateful for all of it. Start to notice how different you feel. It can work whether you want to feel successful, positive, joyful, abundant, wealthy, or literally, any positive emotion you desire can be anchored into you through journaling. Sometimes, your mind may want evidence to back up the journaling. Let's say abundance is something you're working towards and want to embody and feel. Start by journaling about how amazing it feels to be abundant, how grateful you are to be abundant, how much you can do with that abundance, what it looks like, and how it truly feels to be in that vibe. Next, find the evidence of where you're abundant already.

The best place to look is your current surroundings!

Take a look in your cutlery drawer. Or out of your window on a sunny blue-sky day. Look at the number of accounts you can find on Instagram, the number of followers a celebrity has, or the number of loaves of bread in the bread aisle of a supermarket. Abundance is ALWAYS all around you, you've just got to look for it. The more you look for it, the more you will see.

Also, try for a moment to imagine what it will feel like to have an abundance of money if this is your desire.

- Will you never need to worry about filling your car with fuel?

- Will you donate more to charity? How will that feel?

- What about buying gifts and treats for yourself? Will that feel easier?

- Will you feel excited rather than anxious to log into your accounts and check what's in there?

- Will you feel joyful opening your purse or wallet to take money out?

- Will you never need to worry about your direct debits and bills again?

Start to imagine how amazing it will be and feel for you. Really try to connect to those feelings every day. This is what is going to help you feel aligned and ready to receive. Being an energetic match for what you desire. This is where journaling can help you recognise the feeling. You could literally answer all of the questions above as part of your journaling exercise. I'll bet you'll be feeling the feelings after that!

So how can you further anchor into the feeling of something? I love to combine my journaling with meditation or visualisation. I get myself into that desired state through journaling and then close my eyes to do a meditation or visualisation, for no more than 5 minutes. Based on how your mind works, meditation and visualisation are really powerful tools, which we'll get onto later in the book.

When I'm feeling overwhelmed

Journaling is a great way to help you remove the overwhelm you may naturally feel in life, your career, or your business. Sometimes it may feel like things are too much like you have so much on your plate that you don't know how to move forward. This is another area where journaling can truly help you thrive.

I remember one difficult Monday morning in February 2020. I usually love Mondays. Since creating my dream business, I'm so excited to reconnect with clients after the weekend and get myself set for a super week ahead. Yet this one felt really different. I felt off. I couldn't pinpoint what felt wrong, I just didn't feel like me. There was no spark, no passion, no high vibey-ness, and no motivation. Just nothing. I didn't feel ill, or sick, it just felt like I had an internal block.

I tried to do my morning routine, but my mind just felt amiss. It felt a mix of being vacant and disinterested. I went to feed my horse and sort him out, as I do every morning. I spoke to Si briefly, who definitely knew something was up. Despite asking me, I told him I was fine, as I didn't know why I felt the way I did. I carried on with my tasks, and mid-way through doing my jobs, I just burst into tears. It came out of nowhere and they just wouldn't stop. This was a telling sign, but I still wasn't sure of the cause.

I finished up with my tasks, went home, still crying, and wrote a list. I just let my hand write whatever came up in my mind, with no thoughts, judgement, or control. On that list, I put anything and everything that was upsetting me.

There were 11 things on that list. Ranging from big tasks, such as people owing me money, to small tasks, such as needing to order dog food. Just after writing the list, I journaled on what had come up, the fact that I was feeling a little out of control, and that it was all just a bit much for me. I now realise that I actually felt overwhelmed. The release from just writing my list, and categorising what I had control over versus what I didn't was immense. I instantly felt lighter, more free, and was able to regain my control, my motivation, and my mind.

The feeling of overwhelm isn't uncommon. It creeps up in our daily lives, as we take on new projects, push ourselves, or if we have a lot going on. It's so normal to feel overwhelmed, so having ways in which you can handle and manage it is key to your success and happiness.

When I feel I've lost the connection to my why

If you're a business owner, you'll understand how it can be all too easy to get knocked off course. It's easy to get hung up on signing clients, making money, or your launch, creating the right content, and so many other things. Connecting to your why, your vision, or your mission, is a really great way to help you re-focus on the bigger picture.

I've noticed a number of times in my business where I've lost my connection to my why, and I've been too focused on numbers, sales, or signing clients. What normally happens when I recognise this, is that I'm then operating from a place of lack. If I'm just focused on the numbers in my bank, or of sales and clients, all I'm focusing on is that there isn't enough of that thing. When I'm focusing on not having enough, I'm totally in a negative, lack-based energy and vibe. This is when I connect to my bigger mission, which is to help 1,000,000 people with their mindset by 2025. Connecting to my mission helps me think bigger for the long-term, and think about how I can impact others. I'm obsessed with the work I get to share with my audience and clients. It inspires me to keep going, keep elevating, and keep showing up.

Connecting to your why will support you if you have lost your way, motivation, inspiration, or your drive. It happens, but having a way to help you reconnect is key. So for me, when I journal to reconnect with my why, I will ask myself things like why do I do what I do, what do I love most about what I do, who needs me on top form today, how can I best show up to support my audience today, or what magic could I help someone create today. Then, I'm totally connected to my why, to help people create their own dream life and business.

When your mind feels full

We are more online than ever before. Our minds are busier than ever before. We've got more to deal with and process than ever before. There's more external pressure than ever before. It's a lot for your mind to comprehend and deal with.

Journaling is a great way to empty your mind. You see your mind can only ever be 100% full, like a full glass of water. You can't mound the water up, as you could with something that has a firmer consistency, such as mashed potato. Your mind is exactly the same. Yet we are asking more and more of our minds, to remember and do so many things.

Use journaling as a way of clearing everything out. Look at what you are trying to hold onto and remember every day. There may be many things that you don't need to remember. Perhaps you could use a reminder app on your phone to remind you to do something, such as recurring household tasks or tasks for business or place of work. Perhaps you could create a more efficient schedule, such as having set days/times to do admin work, your food shop, learning, or your finances. Perhaps you realise some tasks are so tiny that you could do them now, then they're done. The aim is that you have some awareness of what's going on in your mind so you can further take control and ensure your mind is full of thoughts and things that will support you.

Another thing to recognise based on the assumption that your mind can only ever be 100% full, is that you need to acknowledge what is actually in there. If your mind is full of negativity, fear, worry, or anxiety, there is actually less space for joy, abundance, optimism, and happiness. So, get really honest with yourself here. Are the negative unwanted feelings and emotions taking up too much vital space? If you removed those unwanted thoughts and feelings, what could you put in there instead? More self-belief? More gratitude? More high vibeyness? More goals and dreams? More confidence?

Give your mind a regular clear out, much like you do with the rubbish in your home, and then be mindful of what you *let* back in.

If somebody makes you feel like crap, or their beliefs bring you down, do a little journaling mind-empty and then put some good stuff back in! You've got this!

When I feel my mindset has slipped

Awareness is key for every area of your mindset journey. The journey never stops. There is no start date and end date. This is lifelong work, that you get to enjoy and that changes your life.

Occasionally things may happen, both in and out of your control, that knock you off kilter or make you question yourself. This is totally normal. It's so very easy for your mindset to slip and start making you question yourself once again. It only takes one negative review, a failed launch, or not getting a promotion in your workplace to make you question yourself and not feel good enough. It only takes one direct debit to bounce back, or a late credit card payment to make you feel like you're shit with money. It only takes one minor fuck up for your mind to go into beating yourself up mode. This is totally normal. Your mind will think that being self-critical or negative, it's keeping you safe. That is just not the vibe.

Journaling is a great way to help you recognise how you're feeling and bring you back into a great space. Journaling will bring awareness to everything you've got going on and the thoughts and emotions you're feeling. If you feel like your mindset has slipped, you can ask yourself questions such as how do I feel, why do I feel this way, what's bringing these feelings up, what caused this, and is this a feeling I require? Once you have that awareness, you can flip the inner story by asking yourself questions such as, how do I wish to feel, where has my mindset supported me in the past, what am I proud of, and what am I pleased that I get to do in my life and business.

Journaling enables you to pick apart what's going on, recognise an area of focus or improvement, and act as a tool to help you constantly connect to what you desire. Use it as a safe space for personal development and shifting your thoughts and way of thinking.

Task

1. Grab a notepad or your journal and ask yourself these questions: how do I feel today, how do I wish to feel, what am I excited about, what am I proud of, and what feeling do I desire in life? There is no judgement here, the first step is having the awareness of what's going on internally.

2. Set yourself a goal to journal every day for five days. It may feel weird at first, but do stick with it and try alternative types. Perhaps one day try to get yourself into a desired state, another day might be to decompress and empty your mind, and another day maybe if you're feeling a bit off or overwhelmed. See it as a way of emptying your mind and then putting back into your mind thoughts and feelings that will serve you.

3. Recognise any time anything feels like too much or brings your vibe down. Grab that pen and get journaling! You've got this.

CHAPTER 12

VISION BOARD

Much like with journaling, I didn't actually know what a vision board was until I fell into the world of mindset work. Yet I now use them as a powerful tool to help me create my dream life and business.

Vision boards, also known as dream boards or mood boards, are a powerful way to connect to your goals and what you truly desire.

A vision board is simply a collection of images, words, thoughts, and feelings of what you desire for your future, whether that's a month from now, or your dream vision ten years from now. You might create one for your business or job, for your home, health, or holidays. There really is no right or wrong way there is only what you wish to do and what works best for you.

The reason they work exceptionally well is that your subconscious mind loves pictures and feelings. It can't register or cope with strategies or 'how to's.' It just fails to comprehend them. But it can align with a collection of pictures on your vision board and the associated feelings you expect to feel when you have or create that thing.

This is where your mind not knowing the difference between reality and what you tell it can really be a huge asset. If you connect with your vision board in such a manner that you can imagine having the things on it and can feel the feelings of having those things, then your mind will just assume it's your reality. If your mind can feel the feelings and imagine that this is your reality right now, then that's actually going to give it a boost of confidence to keep working towards that thing. Anything seems possible, especially once you've done it for the first time. If your mind assumes that those things you imagine are real, it'll have your back even more as you work towards creating this into your existence.

The most important thing to consider when looking at your vision board is that you can connect with some of the pictures on such a level that you truly can feel the feelings of already having what you desire in your reality. I have more than twenty pictures on mine, so as part of my morning routine each day, I connect to approximately five pictures. When I say connect to, I mean that I look at that picture, I feel the feelings, I imagine experiencing that thing, and try to feel the total joy I'll get from having it in my life. Sometimes I can do that by gazing at the picture, sometimes I look at the picture as a prompt and then close my eyes and visualise the thing or experience on my vision board.

So if I had a picture of a beautiful beach in the Maldives on my vision board, I would focus on it with my undivided attention. I would imagine landing in the seaplane in paradise. I'd imagine the warmth of the sand between my toes, and the ice-cold cocktail I'd be handed. My time spent sunbathing on the perfect beaches, gazing out at the calm turquoise sea, seeing nothing in front of me but an endless expansive Indian Ocean. I'd imagine how I would feel knowing I manifested this, and that it had been my dream for some time. I'd imagine Si and I going out for dinner to the divine buffet restaurants, sitting by the ocean, feeling the warmth of the ocean breeze on my skin. I would imagine taking pictures of my bright orange cocktails against the blues of the sea. I would imagine laying on the beach, with nothing to do and no worries. I wouldn't even be on tech or reading, I would just be laying there, anchored in gratitude, and paradise.

I get that picture and feel it so clearly and intensely in my mind that I can literally feel the excitement brewing in my body! To help me get clear on that feeling, I have spent a fair amount of time searching for pictures, looking at sandbanks, reading reviews, finding pictures of similar things on social media, and watching promotional videos, where I see the seaplane coming into land at a jetty on one of the beautiful islands. I'm a very visual person, so I do all I can to help myself connect with the feelings and truly imagine how it would look, be, and feel.

Similarly, if I had a picture of the car I wanted on my board, I would imagine how it would feel to go and test drive it, order my chosen specification, and then go and buy it, brand new, from the garage. I would feel the excitement of paying the money, getting the keys, sitting in it for the first time, and starting the engine to drive it out of the showroom. How it would feel to see it parked on my drive, to walk out to it and start it up. How it would feel to drive it, and the massive smile on my face. How it would feel to turn up at a meeting in it. How it would feel to go out for a drive on a sunny day. I even imagine the songs I'd listen to on its epic sound system. I imagine how it would feel to not have to worry about it breaking down, or to feel anxious about putting it through its MOT. For years, I felt sick whenever I took a car for its MOT, as I feared it would cost more to fix than it was worth, or that I had in my bank. That feeling of peace of mind was so big for me and kept me so focused and committed when I was manifesting my car.

Imagining these scenarios for both of the above situations really helps me connect to the feelings of how I'll feel when I get those things. Even just typing those examples out has literally got me mega excited for my next fast car and next trip to the Maldives and I don't even have my vision board in front of me!

The first vision board I created was just before New Year's Eve of 2018. I had been working on my mindset for a couple of months. I heard so many things about them but as with the mindset work, I thought it was a bit 'woo' for someone like me. Nevertheless, after encouragement from my coach, I made my first one.

I did put the Maldives on there and a brand-new Audi S3. At the time, I was yet to have my first £10k month and didn't have a penny of savings, so I had absolutely no idea HOW I would possibly pay for either of those things. But I kept wishing, dreaming, feeling, and connecting with my beautiful vision board every morning. I felt so excited about the possibility, that I started looking at holidays, searching for pictures online, and watching stunning promo videos from some of the many Maldivian islands. I watched car review videos and started looking at the statistics of the car I wanted. I was truly obsessed. I went for a test drive before I was ready and just knew there was no going back.

I will genuinely never forget that test drive. I had already driven an S3 before as my husband had one when we first met - it was partly what made me want to speak to him and as a car lover, I just adored it. I loved when he let me drive it. I felt so special and loved every second of being behind the wheel. But getting into a brand new one that hits 60 mph quicker than most cars can hit 30 mph was awesome! What was really strange was that when I got into the car and sat behind the wheel for the first time, it actually felt exactly as I had imagined. Every time I looked at my vision board, I imagined that exact feeling. It was uncanny. As we pulled out of the garage, I couldn't stop smiling. I was genuinely like a little girl at Christmas who had received everything she asked for. I smiled the whole way around - it was a massive upgrade compared to my ten-year-old A3.

Since putting the S3 on my vision board, I was suddenly seeing them everywhere. I could barely go out in my old car without passing one. Were they suddenly more popular, I thought to myself?

I actually loved seeing them more regularly because every time I saw one, I imagined myself driving it. I would literally say out loud "come on universe, work your magic for my S3!" I would even say it with Si or my friends in the car - I'm sure they thought I was losing the plot! I saw it as a sign from the universe that it was coming, that she was trying to align to help me manifest that car!

The truth is, there were no more S3's on the road than there were six months earlier. I became more aware of them thanks to the visualisation work I had done. My subconscious mind was so obsessed, excited, and connected to the thought of having one, it was always on the lookout for them. I had activated the Reticular Activating System (RAS), the search engine of my mind. Once activated, through visualisation, the RAS will be on the lookout for ways to bring your desires into your reality.

This is why it's so important to focus on what you want rather than what you don't want. Your RAS will be activated regardless, so if you're choosing to focus on things you don't want such as:

- I don't want to be in debt anymore
- I don't want my car to break down
- I don't want to become ill

That's what it's going to start looking for. Your mind fails to comprehend the word 'don't' or 'not', so you need to ensure your thoughts, wishes, and desires are truly in line with what you WANT rather than what you don't want.

So my focus on the car was very much "I want an S3" and "I'm grateful to have a brand new S3" and my subconscious mind and RAS were on high alert to bring that into my reality.

That's the beauty of manifestation and using a vision board. When you can get your mind obsessed with what you want, and you look at that vision board daily, you feel the feelings of having that thing and truly believe it is possible for you. Your subconscious mind will do its best to bring it into your reality. It always wants to give you what you ask of it. It is always listening, learning, and trying to please. We as the creators of our lives, just need to be mega careful of what we wish for! That's exactly why I was spotting the S3's more often. It's the same when you decide to go do something, buy something, or go somewhere, and then you suddenly see that everybody is doing that, buying that, or going there!

As I am editing this part of this book, I've actually owned my S3 for over 3 and a half years and the truth is, I still love it as much today as I did that first day. It honestly makes me so happy and always continually reminds me of my powers as a creator and helps me hold the belief that anything is possible. Tara from just a few years prior couldn't even imagine having such a beautiful, brand-new, fast car. It wasn't part of my reality and I didn't see how it could be part of my future. But I trusted myself to dream. And I think that makes it even better. It makes me appreciate it more. It makes me realise that anything truly is possible.

Because I wanted this car so much and I regularly visualised the feelings of driving and having it, I truly felt that I anchored a feeling into the driver's seat. In the world of NLP, anchoring refers to the process of combining thoughts or feelings with a trigger or stimulus. I had visualised the feeling of being in that driver's seat so much and how I would feel to such an extent that when I get in there, I always feel that way. I have truly anchored the feelings of joy, gratitude, abundance, goal-hitting, prosperity, positivity, and possibility to the driver's seat. So every single time I get in, start the engine and choose my tunes for the drive, I feel those exact feelings.

My husband must get bored with me telling him how much I love it! But I truly do, and that constant feeling of love, happiness, and success obviously continues to anchor and bring more into my life, as what I focus on continues to expand.

When I look back over the past few years to acknowledge what I've hit off of my vision board and how far I've come, I do truly recognise the steps that I have taken to get here. For example, whenever I used to see a young woman driving a nice car, I always assumed it was a company car or her husband's car. That was how closed my mind was, how limited my views were, and how I didn't realise that young women could create their destiny.

Use your vision board as a way to regularly connect with what you actually want. Think of things, words, feelings, emotions, places to visit, experiences you desire, charity donations you may wish to make, the business you desire, or the dream job you'd love. Have fun with it. And dream big, as it takes no more to dream big than it does to dream small.

There will of course be some action on your part in terms of bringing these manifestations into your reality, but it really is amazing what your subconscious mind can do for you when you start connecting to what you desire. You may see things aligned with what you want, you could manifest opportunities, or you might mention something to a friend that may align with what you desire. Trust yourself, have some fun with it, and get ready to manifest some magic.

Task

1. Create your own vision board!

Think about:

- Things you want in your home or office
- Any clothes/outfits you like
- If there's a particular pair of shoes, perfume, a bag you'd like
- If you like a certain brand of candle or diffuser
- What drinks do you like
- Places you'd like to visit
- Recreational activities such as sports, spa days, or walking
- Experiences you may want to enjoy
- Certain rewards for hitting your goals, which we'll dive into in the next chapter!

2. Then print it out and put it somewhere you can either see it daily or include it as part of your morning routine and look at it daily.

3. Remember, the feelings are SUPER important - make sure you feel the feelings of how you'll feel when you get that thing, each time you look at the board.

4. Update as regularly as you need to! I update mine every 2 - 3 months as I continually get things from it.

CHAPTER 13

GOALS

Goals are one of my favourite things. I truly believe they give you total focus, something to work towards, and a guilt-free reason to buy your own rewards and gifts!

It wasn't until I hit rock bottom in April 2017 and started working with a coach that I actually started setting goals. Before that, I was just happy with whatever came in. I didn't really have a lot of visibility on my finances, what I was making, or what I wanted to make. I was just head down, working one day to the next, and signing new clients when they came my way.

I was being reactive rather than proactive.

Until I nearly lost it all.

When I started working with my first coach, she asked me what I wanted to make in a month. I had no idea. I thought back to my first 18 months of business and realised I had a couple of £4k months, and they felt really good for me. I remember at the time being in total awe of the fact that I was making more than double what I used to get paid when I had a managerial role in the hospitality sector. The strangest thing was that I just loved what I was doing. Who knew that was even possible? At the time I was active on social media, writing articles, and interviewing some of the world's leading horse riders at events. I was getting paid SO well for it. It just felt like a dream. I loved earning more and not having to worry about how I was going to pay for food, pay my bills, and pay for an occasional dinner out.

So I told my coach that I'd love to get back to that point. Suddenly, I had my first 'real' goal - to bring in £4,000 in a month. That first session was very much about the strategy and the 'how' of hitting the goal. I didn't know mindset work existed at the time and didn't understand the importance of setting and then feeling the goal. Even so, I felt excited about it and subconsciously found myself imagining it happening. I really feel the imagination piece planted the seed. I remember driving home from that coaching session and just feeling so excited for my future. There and then, in that moment, I knew I'd never let anything, or anyone take my business away from me.

In the summer of 2017, with a strategic plan, a bit of self-belief, some updated packages, rather than relying on pay-as-you-go clients, and a reignited love of my business, I actually hit that £4k goal fairly quickly. I was showing up on social media daily, I was promoting what I did on social media, as well as asking current clients for recommendations and reviews. I shared my client's results and some of my personal results too. I was getting myself out into the big wide world, going to events, and networking, to continue building my confidence. I was constantly learning more, pushing myself out of my comfort zone, and basking in the celebration of hitting these new milestones in my business. Having hit that income level before, I knew I could do it again, especially with a slightly different model. That evidence really helped. Then, I soon increased the goal to a £5k month and had consistent £5k+ months. I suddenly realised I was pretty good at setting and smashing goals! Since then, I've gone on to set and subsequently smash some rather unrealistic goals, including my first 6-figure month, manifesting our dream farm, dream office, successful launches, and finishing this book!

The thing to mention with those larger goals is that I couldn't have predicted those in 2017 when I first started setting goals. I didn't know goals of that size, scale, or possibility existed. I didn't know it was possible for someone like me. I think that's an important point to mention. In talking about these goals or showcasing examples, the numbers might not be relatable for you or feel achievable, and that's fine. Use them as an example and change the numbers to reflect what feels better for you.

Over time, I have tested what I feel works when it comes to setting and smashing goals and I'm excited to share that with you now! In 2021, I developed and trademarked a five-step proven GOALS methodology and framework that I use myself and guide clients through. It has five easy-to-follow steps that can be used time and time again to hit any goal of any size.

So here goes...

1. Go for the goal!

This has to be YOUR goal. Nobody else can set your goal for you. I can't set your goal for you. Neither can your mentor, your family, your partner, or your business bestie. It has to come from you. It's the same with your pricing, which also has to come from you. If it comes from somebody else there will be a disconnect and you won't believe in it, and therefore won't hit it. If you're really new to setting goals and want to start with a financial goal, take a look at what you've made in a month so far and you can either see if you can match it again, or you can see if you want to push it a little. It really is your goal, so see what feels best for you.

2. Own your goal!

Let it sit with you for a while. Do you feel aligned with it? Does it excite you? Do you feel it's possible and do you believe you can do it? In the early days, I would let mine sit with me for about a day and then commit to it entirely. Now, I just know. As soon as a goal comes to mind, I trust that it has come from my gut and that it is my calling. I lean into it and connect to it.

3. Act as if!

This is a key part of goal smashing and really aligns with the journaling exercises we've mentioned and the power of visualisation. If you had already hit the goal, how would you feel? Would you show up a little more confidently online? Would you feel proud of yourself? Would you feel abundant and capable? Would you feel like you show up from a place of calm and intentionality? Start to feel these feelings around the goal that you have set. Feel them regularly, so you can keep tapping into that desired state, then take action from that space. Make sure that the energy around the goal is one of gratitude so you aren't coming at your goals from a negative energy of lack. Do go back to chapter nine if you need a refresher on gratitude.

4. Live the goal!

This is where you take your inspired action. Note that the first 3 of 5 steps are all around your mind, your mindset, and your energy. It's only the last two steps that are action based. Living the goal is about taking action that is aligned with what you want. A lot of people get stuck in fear here. They recognise what they don't want and then take action from that place. The aim is to take an inspired action that is in alignment with what you desire. So for example, if the goal is to sign some high-level clients, the action needs to align with them. The action is not endless scrolling on social and creating content for beginner businesses. Similarly, if you want a promotion or pay rise at work, the action that will increase the chances of that happening will be going above and beyond. Getting yourself in the right spaces and rooms to have that conversation and actually putting yourself forward. Make sure that your inspired action aligns with what you want. Then, keep believing it's working out, even when it looks like it isn't happening or hasn't worked yet. All of the preparations you've put in are manifesting even if they haven't done so yet. Hold the belief!

5. Smash the goal!

How great will it feel to smash the goal!? Keep feeling those feelings. What is your reward for hitting the goal? This is key as it'll help you hit your goal next time. Time and time again I hear of people setting goals, smashing their goals then not rewarding themselves, and wondering why it all came crashing down or was really hard to hit again. Get yourself a reward, even if it's a fancier bottle of wine than you normally drink or a new set of sharpies. It doesn't have to be a massive deal, it can be anything, the point is you're setting the intention and congratulating yourself when you hit your goals. As you get comfortable smashing your goals, you can stretch your goals and stretch the reward you get yourself. More on that later in this chapter.

Throughout all of these steps, the paramount piece is…

Believe, believe, believe.

This is VITALLY important. We've already established that what you believe is what you achieve. If you haven't yet, I urge you to write that out somewhere so you can see it daily. Grab it as your new mantra, repeat it to yourself regularly, and never stop remembering it is so key to your growth in terms of your mindset. If you don't believe you can hit your goal, you won't. It is that straightforward. You've got to truly believe it deep down. You can say all the affirmations, journal on it, and have your vision board but if there is any subconscious block or belief that you can't hit it, you won't. This is where I believe feeling the feelings of hitting the goal works really well as that will trick your mind into believing you've already hit the goal. And if you can trick your mind into believing that, then, what will happen? You will achieve it!

"What you believe is what you achieve."

Once you have the key steps of the methodology clear in your mind, it's important to see or connect with the goal regularly. It is said that the difference between millionaires and billionaires is that millionaires write their goals out daily, while billionaires write them out twice a day. Now I know that is an extreme example and probably totally not relatable for you, but if it's good enough for them, then it's good enough for us! I've been writing out my goals every single morning as part of my morning routine since October 2018, and I have consistently hit them. I feel it starts your day with purpose and intention and gives you such focus. Plus, it keeps you excited, (hopefully, if not, your goal needs pushing!) and continually striving forwards.

As part of the methodology, I mentioned the importance of setting yourself a reward for hitting the goal. This is why that piece is so important.

Imagine when you were younger, that your parents set you a little challenge or a task. Or that you were taking part in the school sports day and won your race. A part of you would expect something, perhaps some sweets or pocket money. Or at the very least, some praise. If you tried your hardest and had nothing, you would feel rather deflated. It may also prevent you from trying so hard or putting in so much effort when you do it next time, because what is the point when you get nothing for your efforts? The same applies when it comes to setting goals. When you set a goal and give it your all, you really should celebrate it when it gets here. Whether it's treating yourself to something new for your home, or taking yourself out for lunch, or a massage, you really need to do something that acknowledges your hard work and success in smashing your goal.

This is actually a mistake I made when I had my first £10,000+ month. The last day of the month was a Friday, and that particular Friday I was at a horse show, and then I had a meeting with a potential client early that Friday evening. I signed two new clients that day and the month of May finished at over £12,000. I made the ninety-minute drive home after my final meeting and arrived at 9:00 pm. I was shattered. May had been a busy month and having left early that morning and driven well over 100 miles I was just ready to crash into bed. June 1st was on a Saturday, and I had a fairly busy weekend. Mondays are always busy for me and then the week can easily get away with me, so by the time I got around to thinking about what had worked well in May and what my goal for June would be, we were a third of the way through the month.

I didn't celebrate my first £10k month and I then didn't set any goals for the next month. June and July of that year were horrendous months from a sales and business perspective.

I had wrongly assumed that because I had had a £10k+ month that it would just naturally keep happening and my money worries would be over. That July of 2019 was the last time I felt so sick around money. It was a real turning point when I knew I had to get better with my money and do some serious money mindset work, so I started working with a money mindset coach alongside the business coaching mastermind I was in.

When I started working with her, I told her I wanted to work towards consistent £15k months, so I set myself a goal of having three consistent £15k months for the twelve-week period I was working with her. My reward? My first pair of Christian Louboutin heels. Those stunning red-soled beauties appeared on my vision board, and I got to work.

Every morning when I looked at them on my vision board, I imagined how I would feel to go in and buy them. To wear them. To see them in my closet. I imagined how I would feel wearing them out for drinks, or dinner, knowing that they were a premium designer product. It made me feel really proud - even if nobody else knew that they were a premium product, it would feel really good knowing I had created this abundance.

Well, the three months flew by! They were totally transformative. And I'm pleased to say, I hit that goal with ease and flow.

When it came to buying my reward, I hesitated. I kept going on to the website to make the purchase and the thoughts of "who am I" to have these shoes that cost THAT much kept coming in. I didn't even feel safe and confident enough to go into a store to buy them in case my card was declined, or someone saw me, hence looking to buy them online. It genuinely took me two months to buy them, and I will never forget the day I did.

I was heading to London to have lunch and drinks with some of the girls in the mastermind I was in. I got on the train for the journey and felt excited the whole way there, knowing I was going to go and buy them in person and that we were going for lunch at one of my favourite venues in London, Sky Garden. When the train stopped at Paddington Station, I hopped on the tube and made my way towards Knightsbridge before getting off and walking into Harrods.

After the initial fear of "who am I to be shopping in Harrods", I stepped forward through the big, heavy, deep green doors.

Now for those of you that have been to Harrods, you'll know how massive it is. It's not easy to find anything other than the food hall, so I asked for directions to the Louboutin store. I must have asked four or five people that worked there - it genuinely is like a maze in there.

Eventually, I got to the store. I recognised the flashes of red a mile off. As the imposter syndrome tried to set in, I put her back in her box and walked proudly into the store, my head held high.

I was in awe at the beauty of some of those heels. They were all so intricately designed, with subtle yet stunning characteristics. Having struggled to find the store, I was running a little behind on time which was probably a blessing as I could have tried on every single pair of shoes! But I knew which pair I wanted. A simple black suede pair that I knew would not only go with the outfit I had on that day but most other outfits too.

I asked the assistant if I could try them on. They hugged my feet and genuinely made me feel like a million dollars. I told the assistant that I'd love to buy them, and he took them over to the checkout for me. When I was there, I was asked "is this your first pair of Louboutin's?" "Yes," I proudly replied, knowing that it wouldn't be my last!

Walking out of that store with a pair of Louboutin's was one of my proudest moments. I actually felt myself stepping into my next level.

I then hopped back on the tube and made my way to Monument Station, carrying that beautiful, branded bag carefully while feeling a real sense of achievement.

As I arrived at our lunch venue, I slipped out of my flat shoes and put my heels on. Sky Garden is a wonderful tourist destination and home to the highest garden in London. It's a truly stunning building with bars and restaurants on the higher of its thirty-seven floors. It has panoramic views of the city, exquisite food and drink offerings, and a real charm about it. It felt like the perfect place to christen my beautiful new heels.

Since then, I have worn them on a whole host of different occasions. Throughout the lockdowns I even wore them around the house in the evening, mincing around in a pretty dress while having Chinese takeaway and Champagne! They are just a vibe. The beautiful thing is, every time I wear them, I remind myself of smashing my goal. I remind myself that anything is possible. I remind myself that I am worthy. That I can keep little miss imposter syndrome in her box. I remind myself of possibilities. And the beauty of it is, it all happens subconsciously!

As with mindset work, the work around your goals is ongoing. It isn't enough to set it, say it once, and get on with your day. Sure, that strategy might work for you on the odd occasion, but for consistent goal-smashing, you will struggle.

When you start setting goals, there will most likely be times when you don't hit them and it's really easy to feel deflated. Despite being the goal-smashing queen, I have been there on the odd occasion too!

It's really important after setting a goal that whether you smash it or not, you take a moment to reflect at the end of the month on the following points, these make great journaling prompts too:

- Was I truly committed to my goal?

- Did I believe my goal was possible?

- Did I connect to my goal every single day?

- Did I take the inspired action to help my goal manifest in my reality?

- What could I have done better?

I also want to say this. You are great at what you do, whether you hit the goal or not. You are worthy as a human, whether you hit the goal or not. There simply cannot be an attachment to how good, worthy, successful, and confident you are based on whether you hit the goal or not. That is not the vibe. You have a vibe, whether you hit the goal or not.

It's also important to mention the importance of being aligned with your goal. I actually talk about alignment in episode 62 of my podcast, Tara Talks. So often I hear from people who see others online smashing £xxk months in their business and they assume that should be a goal they work towards as well. The problem with this is that it's going to be misaligned. It's the same reason I, or your coach, mentor, or business bestie can't set a goal for you. It has to truly come from you.

When a goal is misaligned, there will be a disconnect with your subconscious mind, which will naturally create a disconnect with the universe. You have got to truly and deeply believe in this goal, believe you can have it, know that it is coming to you, and keep working towards it until it does.

Ways your goal might be misaligned with you:

- You didn't put any thought into it

- You set it based on what others are doing

- It's too much of a jump up on your past goals/highest money months

- You didn't believe it was possible for you

One other thing to mention is the time delay.

Sometimes when you set yourself an income goal for a month, you work toward it each day, feeling totally committed and believing it's yours, and then for whatever reason, it still doesn't come off and you're left feeling disappointed and let down. The thing is, there can be a time delay when it comes to goals and manifestation. The Universe has to align itself to your desires and sometimes that takes time. It may be a stretch for the Universe to do that in 31 days or less. Sometimes it might just be testing you to check that you're ready for it. So if you don't hit that specific income goal in the month you desire, I would suggest you keep working towards that specific goal and just remove the time frame, because if you give up after one month then that is setting a really poor intention to the Universe. The Universe wants to give you what you want but sometimes it just takes a little time.

As with everything in this book, it takes time to get into the swing of things when it comes to goals. It's about finding your way, and finding what works best for you when it comes to hitting goals and continually trusting that it's coming. Have some fun with the goals, after all, life's too short not to!

Task

1. Set yourself a goal. I would push it a little in terms of what you've achieved so far - whether it's an income goal, savings goal, or health goal.

2. What is your reward *when* you hit your goal?

3. Get your reward and goal on your vision board.

4. Write it out each morning as if it's already happened such as "I am so grateful for my £3k month!" Feel the feelings when you write it out of how you'll feel when you smash it! Will you want to squeal with joy? Will you do a happy dance? Who will you tell? How will you feel when you purchase your reward? Connect to all of those feelings (you can actually connect to those feelings in a matter of seconds - that is enough!)

5. Take inspired action. Continue to go about your day believing in it. Remember, what you believe is what you achieve. You've GOT to believe you can do it, otherwise, you won't.

6. Let me know when you hit it. And make sure you celebrate it!

CHAPTER 14

MEDITATION AND VISUALISATION

When I was first encouraged to try meditation, I thought my coach was joking. Or at least trying to push her jet-set ways and tendencies onto me.

At the time I was working towards my first six-figure year and quite frankly, I didn't see how that was going to help me hit that goal. I also didn't have the time to meditate and felt my mind was too busy to actually meditate - both were signs that I needed to do it!

You see, my view of meditation was very stereotypical. I thought that it was very monk, Buddha style - sitting with crystals, with your legs crossed and humming.

In the early days, I tried a number of different ways. I tried listening to a guided meditation on YouTube while laying down in the morning but found myself just falling back asleep. I tried sitting there at the kitchen table meditating with my eyes closed but felt so awkward and I just kept opening my eyes. Then I decided to light a candle and gaze softly, with the guided soundtrack playing quietly. That worked! I was able to focus on the gentle flicker of the flame while focusing on my breathing and the guidance in the clip that was playing.

As with anything, particularly parts of a morning routine, it took time to build it into my routine and form it as a habit. It felt like I was doing it for a long time before I noticed any huge difference. But, with my coach for accountability, I kept going.

The more I look into the mind, how it works and the habits of high performers and successful people, the more I realise the importance of calming and quieting the mind. And to me, that's the purpose of meditation. However you sit and approach meditation, the aim is to quiet your mind. Other meditative states can include when you're walking, cooking, and falling asleep. It's the point at which you have the sole purpose of quieting your mind.

Our minds are SO busy and dealing with more and more on a daily basis than they were ever designed to. We continue to ask more and more from them, dealing with bigger and more complex issues every day. Our minds and our lives are also more available and active than ever before. Thanks to the plethora of social media apps, accessibility to streaming services, and the 'always online' culture. We're always messaging, always responding, and always available, which means that we're less available for ourselves and prioritising our self-care.

While it is great that we have access to these things and access to technology like never before, it is important that we do also give ourselves a break from tech, life, being, and doing.

That's where meditation (in whatever form that looks for you) can really help. I must confess, this has been the hardest part of the morning routine for me. I have such an 'on' brain, constantly innovating, thinking, dreaming, and creating, so it has been hard to actually switch it off. But there are many benefits and many different ways to do it.

The aim is to always focus on your breathing. Being in control of your breathing helps to calm and quiet the mind. It isn't easy keeping your mind blank - I challenge you to try it and see how long you can last! But giving your mind a focus such as your breathing really helps. When I meditate, I like to do the following breathwork exercise.

---

4 - breathe in slowly for 4 seconds

4 - hold your breath for 4 seconds

4 - exhale slowly for 4 seconds

There are many variations on this, with another popular choice being the 6,2,6 breath pattern (breath in for 6, hold for 2, exhale for 6 seconds) - it really is about finding what works best for you.

When I'm launching something in my business, I incorporate meditation into my morning routine every day as a non-negotiable. I've recognised that it really is important to ensure I have moments of calm throughout my day. I'll also schedule time in my calendar to meditate or visualise at lunchtime, just to reset ahead of the afternoon sessions.

So how can meditation help?

Beyond calming and quieting the mind, practising meditation can significantly improve brain function and energy. In his book *Becoming Supernatural*, Dr. Joe Dispenza states that one of his workshop attendees was able to witness significant changes in her brain, after extended periods of meditation. This brought an increase in energy to the brain, specifically the pineal gland, which is responsible for the production of melatonin. During meditation, your brain waves transition from a normal beta state to a high beta and then a high-energy gamma state. The area surrounding the pineal gland as well as the part of the brain that processes strong emotion is highly activated in this state.

Melatonin is often referred to as the sleep hormone as it is produced at night and regulates your sleep patterns. A lack of melatonin production can reduce your quality of sleep which will have a detrimental impact on your following day.

We've touched on how meditation can help you and the benefits of it, so how is visualisation different and how can that help.

There is a bit of a crossover between the two but they both have a strong purpose in creating your future. To me, meditation is the art of sitting and quieting your mind. Whereas visualisation is the act of actively trying to create an image in your mind based on a desired outcome.

The film, The Secret, explains how visualisation can support the Law of Attraction exceptionally well. You are a magnet, creating and attracting your dream future to you all the time, whether you realise it or not. That's why if you ever find yourself stumbling out of bed in a bad mood, it rarely stops there.

Chances are you will then go on to stub your toe, spill your coffee, run out of milk, and are then late for work as every set of traffic lights on the way turned red as you approached. That initial stumbling out of bed in a bad mood has set your intention for the day and the day then runs YOU, rather than you running it. You let the day happen to you. As everything starts going wrong, there's probably a small part of your mind saying *"oh great, now THIS has gone wrong TOO. Just my luck!"* The universe will only ever give you what you ask for and what you focus on, so as you're complaining about everything going wrong for you, that's what it's going to deliver more of to you.

The same is true when you focus on goodness and the things you desire, which is where visualisation works so beautifully. It gives your mind a focus and sets an intention for the universe. How might your day change and improve if you started each day by getting out of bed and instantly smiling? Then if you feel gratitude for something - whether it's the roof over your head, your health, or your partner or dog next to you. Choose how the day runs for you. And dream big. Make yourself a delicious breakfast and feel full of gratitude, you have a lovely drive to work and are constantly in a state of appreciation, then things are much more likely to go well for you.

You can also visualise how you'd like your day to go. This works particularly well if you're doing something new or challenging, launching something, or going for an interview or promotion.

The reason that visualisation works exceptionally well is because our mind doesn't know the difference between reality and what we tell it. Your mind really can't tell whether the images are real or not. We touched on this a little in chapter 12 when we discussed vision boards. If you can get your mind to see that picture, whether on a vision board or as part of a visualisation and you can connect to the emotion and feelings of it being yours, then it's going to stimulate the Reticular Activating System and help it connect to that goal on an emotional level, and actively search for it.

For years, visualisation has been a key performance tool for professional athletes, musicians, and performers, as they take time to visualise how they want their performance to go ahead of starting their activity.

If it has worked for these sorts of performers, how can we use it in our everyday lives and businesses?

Visualisation aims to take a task, goal, or moment, and picture how it will happen in your mind ahead of time. Instead of just thinking that it goes fine, why not picture it going as well as it possibly can?

Here are some examples of things I visualise:

- Launching a new service and having an inbox full of dream enquiries

- Selling out programmes

- A dreamy day of client calls (I particularly do this if I feel a little overwhelmed ahead of a hectic day!)

· Selling out my retreats

· Seeing a dream potential client say yes on a Zoom call

· Logging on to my online banking apps and my Stripe account and seeing my desired amounts in there.

Spending just a few minutes a day visualising your future will really help - too often we get caught up in the day-to-day of life and business without taking a moment to dream big or aim for what we really desire.

Task

Start having a listen to some visualisations and meditations. Get a feel for what works for you. Consider whether you prefer hearing somebody guiding you through it, or whether you prefer to just hear calming music. Do you prefer male vocals or female vocals? Start with really short (5 minute) soundtracks and start with the intention of just quieting the mind. You may find you feel really calm afterwards, or really relaxed, or you may find that you feel energised and like you have your focus again. There is no one size fits all and no right or wrong answer. So just trust yourself and have some fun with it! You'll also find a guided future self visualisation that I have recorded and added to my website, so do give that a go too! You can find it at www.tarabest.com/book.

PART THREE

CHAPTER 15

HOW CAN A MORNING ROUTINE IMPROVE YOUR SELF-BELIEF?

"Confidence and self-belief can be your superpower. Believe you can and you're halfway there."

I am a massive lover of a motivational YouTube video and I generally listen to one every morning. One of my favourites has an insanely powerful message; "the graveyard is the wealthiest place on the planet because, in the graveyard, you will find dreams that were never followed and ideas that were never invented."

The reasoning for that is largely due to a lack of self-belief. Because it will be that lack of belief that holds people back from trying new things, inventing new things, and giving something a go, even if it scares them. It also holds many people back from setting up their dream business, because their underlying thoughts are "I can't do this" or "who am I to do this" - both thoughts are backed by a lack of self-belief.

Another of my favourite quotes is by the great Henry Ford, *"whether you think you can or you can't, you're right."* If you believe you can do something, you're right. You will do it and you'll thrive. But if you believe you can't do something, then you're also right. This really goes some way to confirm the importance of believing in yourself. If you're wanting to start something or try something new, then the self-belief piece is critical.

This statement from Ford works on an even deeper level than just the belief at surface level. With every thought you have, your subconscious mind will go into its memory bank and find a memory that backs up what that thought is meaning. So if you want to do something, such as set up your own business, and your primary and immediate thoughts are "I can't do that - I'm not confident," then your subconscious mind will find memories to back that up. It will remind you of an event where you tried something new and it didn't work out, as you weren't confident. On the flip side, if you're wanting to set up your business and your thoughts are positive and beneficial for yourself such as "yes, I know I can do this, I'm so excited!" then the subconscious mind will find a memory or multiple memories to back *that* up and will most likely remind you of times where you tried something new and absolutely nailed it! That memory will give you that inner boost of self-belief and confidence that you need to thrive.

The saying *"what you believe is what you achieve"* is critical here as well. As your mind doesn't know the difference between reality and what you tell it, it just believes everything you say. It doesn't even think you could possibly be lying to it. It listens to everything you say and every thought you have and just believes you. If you've been telling yourself something for long enough and you believe it to be true, then that is what you will achieve.

Self-belief (or rather, a lack of it) really is the difference between people who follow their hearts and smash their goal, and those who don't.

Self-belief can be defined as *"a person's belief in their ability to complete tasks and achieve their goals"* - Bandura, 1995. The very definition confirms that if you believe in yourself, you're more likely to hit your goals.

Many studies state that self-belief and inner confidence is not something you are born with. Writing in Psychology Today, award-winning author, keynote speaker, and leader in the field of children's emotional health, Maureen Healy, states that it is very much a skill to be mastered. She calls believing in yourself a *skill* - implying that it needs to be learnt and practised regularly to continue to master it.

I truly believe that self-belief and inner confidence have more to do with how you feel internally and the story you're telling yourself than it is about gaining the approval or external validation of others.

Another of my favourite quotes is from David J. Schwartz. In his book, The Magic of Thinking Big he says, *"with self-belief, the "I'm positive, I can attitude generates the power, skill, and energy needed to do. When you believe you can do it, the 'how to do it' develops. Plus, believing you can succeed allows others to place confidence in you which enhances your confidence. Disbelief is a negative power - when the mind disbelieves, it attracts reasons to support this disbelief. Think doubt and fail. Think belief and succeed."*

That paragraph sums up self-belief SO well and even highlights its many benefits. I've read it to most of my clients and even read it out loud at my retreats and on my podcast. The great news is, it is something you can learn and acquire, and it really will be one of the best things when you do.

I think it's also important to mention that even if you are already confident and believe in yourself, there will probably be times when that is challenged, such as when you're stepping out of your comfort zone or trying something new. So it's a great idea to have a little trick up your sleeve to help you in those times of need, which we will get onto later in the book.

So, how does a morning routine help your self-belief?

As we discussed in chapter seven, your mind doesn't know the difference between reality and what you tell it. Unfortunately, if you don't believe in yourself, that's an inner story you've probably been telling yourself for years. In your first hour of waking, your mind is like a sponge and it's in an adaptable state. If you recall, that's when it's in a state similar to your pre-seven-year-old mind - it's highly influential and absorbs everything in the environment. So if self-belief is an area you'd like to work on, then let that be the main focus of your morning routine.

You can use this to your advantage and revolve your morning routine around your desire, in this instance, to believe in yourself more or fully, and then over time, when you commit consistently, you will begin to rewire your belief system. There are several aspects of the morning routine, which we will get into, but if that is your main goal, then you can revolve the entire routine around that.

Task

· Write out a list of your beliefs around your self-belief and confidence.

· Now ask yourself, is this belief really my truth? Do you truly believe it?

· Ask yourself, when did you believe in yourself? When did you feel confident? Is there an area of your life, business, or workplace where you do feel confident or believe in yourself?

· Now try to re-frame it, flip it on its head, and turn it into a positive statement. There is another example below for you.

· Those are your new mission statements and beliefs - read them, write them, and say them daily. Be sure you say them with intention so that you actually believe them. Remember, what you believe is what you achieve!

If one of the beliefs you have is that you're not confident and you recognise this from the above exercise, ask yourself how you can flip it. Could you try "I am confident" as your daily affirmation? If that feels like too much of a stretch right now, you could try "I am working my way to being more confident or confidence is my birthright."

CHAPTER 16

HOW CAN A MORNING ROUTINE HELP YOU FEEL MORE POSITIVE?

Every morning when you wake up, you're starting your day on a fresh slate. You have a new time to shine and thrive. Your mind is exactly the same. For the majority of people who don't yet understand their mind or practice mindset work, they'll wake up and their first few thoughts will be negative.

As humans, we have an average of 70,000 thoughts a day, the majority of which are negative. Reports and studies have found different percentages but an article by Prakhar Verma in Medium stated that 80% are negative and 95% are repetitive thoughts. This figure really struck a chord. You can see how it's really quite easy to stay stuck, to keep thinking the same thoughts, and why it's so easy to get stuck in a negative rut. I would also expect that the repetitive thoughts are the negative ones, keeping you in a negative state of mind.

Now there will be times when things are going wrong in your life, I'm not saying there won't. Being able to start your day the right way, from a positive place really will make you capable of dealing with many situations.

When you start your day with intention, focused on your goals, and how you wish your day to pan out, you're starting it from the best possible place. You're setting yourself up for success and giving yourself the best possible chance, rather than letting the day happen to you.

What I've certainly found with my own morning routine is that the days I don't do it, which are very rare now as I see an immediate change in how I feel when I don't do it, are the days I struggle the most. Stressful situations are more stressful, limiting beliefs are more present, and negative thoughts are more abundant. I have been diligent with my morning routine for over 4 years at the point of writing this.

I actually feel much more optimistic about myself when I've done my morning routine as I have started my day with positivity, focus, and intention, rather than letting the day run me.

In an article in Healthline, writer Adrienne Santos-Longhurst states that in a study of 70,000 women from 2004 to 2012, those that were optimistic had a significantly lower risk of dying from several major causes of death including heart disease, stroke, cancer, infection, and respiratory diseases.

Adrienne also states other health benefits of thinking positively including better quality of life, higher energy levels, better psychological and physical health, faster recovery from injury or illness, fewer colds, lower rates of depression, better stress management, and a longer life span. What's not to like about any of those!?

In his book, *Becoming Supernatural,* Dr. Joe Dispenza states that when you are feeling angry, hurt, stressed, jealous, rage, competition, or frustration, a signal is sent from the heart to the brain which triggers the release of approximately 1,200 chemicals into your body, equal to the feelings you're having. This chemical dump lasts just under two minutes and in short, bursts pose no real threat to your overall being. However, continual negative or down feelings can result in the regular releasing of these chemicals meaning you're constantly living in a survival state.

Long term, this has massive implications, effectively putting your body into a constant state of incoherence, making you much more vulnerable to stress-related health challenges. Referring back to chapter nine, we understand the mind's filtering system, which filters millions of pieces of information and gives you just seven pieces every single second. When you're stuck in a rut, your mind will continue to give you negative thoughts and things to focus on, and you'll quite likely be having those feelings Dr. Dispenza mentioned, of hurt, rage, anger, and stress among others. When you're unable to get yourself out of a negative mindset you have three very powerful issues to contend with - the filtering system, the chemical release in your own body, and the Law of Attraction, which states that what you focus on expands. I really feel this supports the work around enhancing your mindset and proves that it really can help reset not only your internal filter but how your day goes and the overall health of your mind and body.

The aim of the morning routine is to encourage you to get yourself into a positive state, frame of mind, and mindset that will benefit you and your day. This is where things like gratitude, your vision board, and meditation excel - they do truly get you into that positive frame of mind ready for your day.

Task

· Make a table of two columns and list out the negative thoughts and beliefs you currently have in the first column. Be sure to put any beliefs, thoughts, worries, or concerns in the chart. There are some examples below.

· Now in column two, write out a positive reframe for that negative thought or belief. I've shared some examples in the table below.

Negative, unwanted thought	Positive alternative
"I can't do this - it's OK for them because they're further along, had more help, or have more money"	"I can do anything and everything I put my mind to. There is no limit within me other than my mind!"
"I'm so annoyed at this situation right now, if only it were better"	"I'm in exactly the right place in my life right now and everything is working out for the best"
"Who am I to have this successful launch, life, car, or house?"	"Who am I not to, anything is possible for me"

What we've done in the table above is re-framed the negative belief or thought with a positive alternative. It's so easy to let the negative thoughts take over but it's so important that we take control of them and choose to *focus* on the positives in every situation. If you can truly see the good in every situation (there's a challenge for you!), your life will be truly transformed. Personally, that is one of the biggest changes to my own life since doing mindset work.

Another great exercise to help you start to see the positives in more situations, especially less than ideal or slightly negative situations, is to create another chart, laid out as per the below. On one side you write the positives from the day or situation and on the other side, you write the positive *learnings* from the day or situation. The positive learnings are the things that didn't go so well or as planned, and that you can learn from next time. So instead of beating yourself up about something and calling it a negative, you're able to work out and see how you can complete an action better next time. This is to ensure you're always seeing difficult and challenging situations from a better mindset. You want to ensure there are more positives in the right-hand column than positive learnings in the left. Let's assume the launch of an offer in your business didn't go as you hoped, or the meeting at work didn't go very well. It's so easy to dwell on the negatives but that won't help you move forward properly. So instead, look to celebrate what *did* go well, and then look at how you could make the situation even better next time in the positive learnings column.

I've put some examples in the column below based on how I would handle a day, launch, or situation not going as well as I would have liked.

What are the positives about the situation I faced today?	What are the positive learnings from the situation I faced today?
I received some lovely feedback today.	Even though I didn't hit my goal today, I'm pleased to have welcomed such perfect clients into my programme.
I'm so excited to support the clients that signed up.	Maybe I could build better quality relationships with my audience and what that looks like.
I managed my energy and mindset really well today.	There is still plenty of time to sign more clients and help more people.

Take a go with the exercise any time you recognise you feel flat, negative, or deflated when something hasn't gone to plan or as you would have liked. It really will shift your perspective so you can continually move forward and live your life from a positive place.

CHAPTER 17

HOW CAN A MORNING ROUTINE HELP YOU FEEL CALM AND FOCUSED FOR THE DAY?

Brendon Burchard's study of high performers is one of my favourite captivating pieces of research. You may recall we touched on it a little earlier in the book. He spent years researching the minds and habits of some of the world's most successful high achievers and performers to find out what made them and kept them so successful. The findings were recorded in his book, *High Performance Habits*. This is the first book on business that I read in 2018.

He recognised that they all had a morning routine. They started their day with intention, doing things to support their success and help them get to where they want to go. They most certainly didn't start their day in bed scrolling the latest trend on a social media platform.

Now, I know you may be thinking that you might not be at that level (yet!), but just imagine what's possible for you if you start implementing habits that support your mindset and personal development. Regardless of what you do, starting your day with some intentionality and being in control of your own thoughts will help everything go much smoother. I have clients who are busy Mums, as well as business owners who recognise how much easier it is to get the children out of the house in a calmer manner because they manage their thoughts first thing in the morning. If they can do it, imagine how it will set you up for success too!

Starting your day with a morning routine enables you to manage your day and decide how you desire it to go. It will support you in feeling more prepared, productive, and efficient, rather than rushing into your first task with a mind that is totally catastrophizing everything, worrying, and totally making a hell out of heaven.

I notice a real difference in my calmness and focus when I've done my morning routine. For me, the feeling of calm comes from having things organised, feeling like I have a plan, knowing what I have to get done in my day, being in control of my mind, and being my biggest fan.

Those feelings of calm can come from the clarity and intention I get from doing my morning routine. Writing my gratitude list makes me realise I already have so much, which keeps me in a positive and controlled mindset. Connecting to my goals helps me know the steps I need to take towards them without feeling completely overwhelmed. Having clarity over the tasks in my day and what needs to get done helps me recognise I have a clear plan of action. My journaling exercise helps clear the thoughts whirring around my mind. This will be different for every single one of you and every single situation in which you find yourself feeling busy. The aim is that you start your day in a way that supports you and what you're working towards.

There are times when I have so much to do and I find myself feeling that the morning routine is just another thing to do, so I just get started with my day as soon as I wake up. I promise you, on those days when I dive straight in, I feel erratic, stressed, overwhelmed, and panicked and I simply can't function at my best. My clients experience exactly the same.

Even if it's a day off where I'm running lots of errands, or need to be here, there, and everywhere, or where we have lots to do on the farm, spending a few minutes focusing on how well I want my day to go and how I've totally got this really does make the day go smoother. Sometimes as part of that morning routine, I simply check in with my calendar or diary and re-confirm in my mind my timings and what needs to get done, then, of course, I re-affirm that I've got this and that it will all work out!

I think it's really key to focus on your breathing when you feel busy or like you have a lot to do. When you're feeling stressed, anxious, or overwhelmed, your breathing pattern changes. It can become really short, shallow, and purely in the upper chest which actually triggers the stress response in your brain. This stress response is reduced when you engage your diaphragm when breathing, meaning you take longer, slower, deep breaths in. A report on the Better Health Channel highlighted that abdominal breathing helps to control the nervous system and encourages the body to relax, bringing about a range of positive health benefits.

Imagine the difference between going into a busy day feeling calm, in control, and like you've got this versus feeling out of control, overwhelmed, and like you're behind with everything. There is a lot to be said about this in terms of your productivity and even overall enjoyment of your day.

When you focus on the fact that everything will get done, everything will go your way, your mindset and energy are in the right place to get through it all, and you connect with the feeling of accomplishment, your day will unravel beautifully before you!

Task

1. Spend just a few minutes writing out, planning, or thinking about what you have on that day, make yourself a list, if lists work well for you, and get clear on priority tasks.

2. Take a few moments to really ensure you're breathing properly. Are your breaths short and in your upper chest or are they full deep breaths filling your lungs and abdomen? In this instance, I would recommend breathing in for 4 seconds, holding for 2 seconds, and breathing out for at least 4 seconds. Feel your mind, body, and nervous system calm as you do so.

3. Next, how do you want to feel throughout your day? How do you want your day to go? Do you want an easy drive to work? Perhaps you'd like the meeting at work to go well? Or the technology to be on your side? Perhaps it's that the offer you put out for your business is well received. This sounds so basic, but remember, focus on what you want, NOT what you don't want.

CHAPTER 18

HOW CAN A MORNING ROUTINE HELP YOU WITH YOUR INTENTION FOR THE DAY?

We've touched on this already, but genuinely, most people stumble out of bed and allow the day to happen to them. They let their thoughts spiral, they let things happen to them, and they waft through the day with no real intention. I know you're different because you've made it this far in this book! So take a moment to recognise how amazing you are for a hot second...

Now, I truly believe in taking control of your day. This can look different at different times of your life based on what you have going on. Sometimes, it's writing out how you'd like your day to happen, designing how well it can go, and believing fully that you can and will take control of how your day goes. If you have some free or creative time in your day, set an intention that some magic may occur, and set the intention that you can handle any stressful situation that may arise.

Ask yourself this, if you could wave a magic wand how would you want to feel throughout your day? On a day when you have back-to-back meetings. On a day when you want to be creative. On a day when you have a difficult situation to tackle. On a day when you're having some downtime. Simply set the intention you wish to set.

So, for me, if I'm on coaching calls all day, I set the intention that my calls go amazing and I support my clients with positive energy and enthusiasm all day. If I'm launching an offer, I set the intention that technology works well, that I show up with my best level of high vibeyness, and that the offer is super well received. If I'm having a CEO day where I work ON not IN the business, I set the intention that I have plenty of creativity, I get all of my tasks done, and I handle everything I need to handle like a true boss. If I'm having difficult conversations or having to make difficult decisions, I set the intention that I'm a super strong woman, that I've got this, and can handle whatever the day throws at me. So the intention will vary. But it starts with you deciding how you want your day to go and how you want to feel as you move through your day. There is so much power in this!

Your morning routine is YOUR time. Ask yourself this, how *do* you want your day to go? Do you want it to be mediocre? Lacklustre? Boring? Or do you want it to all go as well as it can? Do you want the clients to show up, the traffic lights to be green, or there's no queue at Starbucks!? Seriously have some fun with it!

Here are some journal prompts to consider:

- How do you want to feel today? Happy, joyful, content, proud, supported, empowered, creative, abundant - you choose! Get mega descriptive and just imagine you're writing it out as perfectly as it could be.

- What do you want to go really well today? Do you have meetings? Speaking to a potential client? Perhaps a deadline to work to or a final piece of work to complete? In the ideal world, how would that event go?

- What opportunities would you like today? Do you want that dream enquiry to come through? Do you want an invite to something? Do you want to be given the inspired action to move the needle towards your goals?

Setting the intention in the morning of how you wish your day to go whilst really connecting to your goals does more than just focus your mind. When you can really connect to the vision and mission that you have, it activates the Reticular Activating System, which as we now know, is your mind's own search engine.

Let's say you set an intention to get a new enquiry through social media. In setting that intention and connecting to your income goal or goal of how many clients you wish to support, your subconscious mind will come up with the creative ideas and inspired action you can take to increase your chances of hitting that goal and smashing the intention that you set. As you're going about your day, the creative ideas and inspired action you can take to hit the goal will come flooding in. Now, generally, those ideas come to you when you're doing mundane, repetitive, or easy tasks, such as driving, showering, or walking your dog. They're much less likely to come when you're sitting at your desk trying to think about what you can do to generate sales or enquiries.

Take that inspiration, and always write down or record on a voice recorder any creative ideas that you have that move the needle in your business. Chances are, if you try and remember them, as soon as you're in front of your laptop or notepad, the conscious mind kicks in and the idea you had is gone.

So with the example of having that dream enquiry, your subconscious mind might remind you of someone who enquired a few months ago that you could reconnect with. It might encourage you to go live on social media or to send an email to your list. It's all about setting the intention, letting the inspired action flow, and then taking that inspired action, that will help you get what you desire.

So setting the intention can help move the needle in your business, it can help your subconscious mind work out what it needs to do or launch to increase your chances of hitting that goal or intention.

Task

Practice setting your intention each day! It can be a short sentence or a couple of sentences. It doesn't have to be a massive action, just something that gives you a positive focus and potential of what could happen for your day. Recognise how your morning routine can shift the way you move through your day and the focus you have as you go through life. You can always use the journal prompts above to guide you.

Let's go!

CHAPTER 19

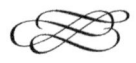

HOW CAN A MORNING ROUTINE HELP YOU FEEL CONNECTED TO YOUR LONG-TERM VISION?

I truly hope by now that you're starting to see the benefits of a morning routine! It genuinely has transformed the lives of me and my clients.

In this chapter, we're looking at how your morning routine can support you with your long-term vision or mission. The truth is, it's so easy to get bogged down in the day-to-day running of life and work, and rarely take the time needed to continue working towards our dream. In fact, a lot of people don't even have a mission. Since working on my mindset and goals, I've had a couple of mission statements. In the early days, it was a simple sentence about how I wanted to feel, how I wanted to show up, and how much I could help my clients. As my company grows, so does my mission statement! An example of my mission statement now is:

CHAPTER 19

"My company is having a massive impact on this world. It continues to ripple out inspiring and motivating people around the globe. It is wildly profitable and manageable in less than 25 hours a week. I have a team of world-class leaders in place that also support my clients. My coaching gives my clients the most epic transformations. They continue to thrive and grow in confidence, while making more money and living their best business life, all with ease and flow. I just love helping these women change their lives."

Whenever I'm feeling flat, lacking motivation, or perhaps feeling misaligned, just reading my mission statement re-aligns me. It reconnects me to my bigger purpose, to my why. Literally just reading that back whilst writing this has brought up a feeling of excitement within me!

Combining your vision or mission statement with things like your vision board, your journaling, and affirmations really will bolster the energy of excitement.

At this point, your vision board is hopefully full of beautiful things, exciting memories you're going to create, and images and feelings of your dream life. Use this to keep you focused on your future best self. What does it mean for you to buy the product you desire? Or to experience that event? Or to hit that goal? Or to manifest the most wonderful things? What will each of those things mean for your life, for your friends, and for your family? I hope when you connect to those images, you are able to feel that excitement!

If any anxious feelings come up about how big your goals or mission are, see how you can turn them into excitement!

Harvard Business School professor Allison Wood Brooks states that anxiety is a negative state of high arousal. Often when we feel anxious our immediate thought or the advice we receive from others is to 'just calm down' but this is in fact the opposite of what you need to do. Allison goes on to explain that calmness is a positive state of low arousal, which is both an extremely difficult and counterproductive state to get into when you're feeling anxiety.

Anxiety itself has a powerful momentum arousal. Her article in *The Business Insider,* Allison states that "this shifts our heart rate, our breathing rate, and activates the release of hormones designed to keep us vigilant, alert and awake."

Getting into a state of calmness with those functions is going to be very difficult. It's also good for us to function with a dose of this arousal in order to perform at our best.

This is where converting that feeling of anxiety to excitement is key. From a physiological perspective, there is very little difference in the brain when you feel both anxious and excited. These two emotions even share a pathway within your mind, meaning your brain doesn't know whether you're anxious or excited. It's the conscious story you tell yourself that helps you determine which feeling it is you're experiencing.

The example Allison used was in regard to thinking about your future. If you think about your future and imagine everything going wrong, it will trigger that thought process in your mind. Your mind will then tell you the story that this is less than ideal and will trigger the reflexes required to stimulate your arousal and make you more alert. However, if you think of your future and visualise the exciting things you want to happen, believe and feel those feelings that everything is working out for you, it will make you feel excited. The difference is the inner story you're telling yourself. In terms of changing how you feel, you're simply changing the narrative of the inner story, not our basic physiology.

I also want to point out that when thinking of your future self, feelings of overwhelm and anxiety should be fairly low. If you're constantly being triggered by them and feeling overwhelmed or anxious, then I would encourage you to journal on these feelings. Is it the case that your vision board or goals have been influenced by somebody? Perhaps they're what you think you *should* be doing, not what you want to be doing? Pressure from yourself is fine, but pressure from others in terms of how you live your life will just result in failure or negativity. Your vision of success and how you want to live is rightfully yours. Trust the desires.

I actually believe that every single morning, your mind is like a blank piece of paper. It's like the first page in a new notepad, clear and ready for you to write your dream day on. Yet so many people just wake up and start with the negative thoughts or the 'doing' of a mundane morning. You have an opportunity every single day to write about your dream day. How do you want to show up? How do you want to feel today? What do you want to achieve today? What is your main goal or intention for today? Use that blank piece of paper that is your rested, morning mind, to create that. Take control of your desires and the outcome of how your day runs. Connecting to your bigger mission in the morning, no matter what it is, will truly help you with that.

Things to consider:

- What small step forward can you take today?
- What opportunities would you like to call in today?
- What can your future self thank you for today?
- How much do you want to enjoy your life today?

These sound like such simple questions and prompts, but just by answering those four, you'll start to create your dream day. Taking control day after day will really show you the difference. I also think it's important to do this both in business and out of it.

I've made the mistake before of not doing my morning routine for a week and I always notice the difference after a couple of days, despite having been doing it for years. When I have time off, my morning routine and intentions are around:

- My business continuing to run smoothly in the background
- Being grateful for the time off
- Being open and ready to receive creative ideas while enjoying myself
- Asking my subconscious mind to make a quantum leap while I'm resting

- Sending positive vibes to my clients and team, to help them recognise they can do anything

---

Even if you go through a tough time, it's SO important to continue writing out how you want your day to go. Let's say you're wiped out with a sickness bug or the flu, start thinking positive thoughts about how you're grateful to get better, and remember to focus on what you want, not what you don't! If you're having a difficult time with a family member or friend, focus on the healing of that relationship or the fact you're grateful to be strong enough to handle whatever life throws at you. You *always* have everything within you to get through whatever life throws at you. Perhaps you have to go and visit a friend in the hospital, be thankful that she's in the best place possible, and start thinking about that easy drive, ease of finding a parking space, and that there isn't a queue at the hospital's coffee shop. What about knowing you have an awkward and uncomfortable call to handle at work or in your business? That would easily flood someone's mind with fear, anxiety, and worry. Focus on the positive outcome you desire, handling it exceptionally well and it going as you wish.

Once you're able to shift your focus for the short-term, such as day-to-day, you can then start to connect to your long-term. This is where your gratitude for what you have now and what you desire, your vision board, your goals, and your visualisation can really support you, as they can purely be focused around the dream life you're creating.

An exercise I love to do that connects me to my long-term vision is to write a future diary entry. This is where you write as if you're writing from a future date, in that future moment. You focus on what you can see, hear, and smell, who is with you, how you feel, what is happening, and any other details that help you really visualise or feel it.

In November 2019, I did this exact exercise, writing out how it would feel to have manifested us moving into the exact dream farm we wanted. I wrote about being stood in the kitchen, the candles I could smell, the Champagne I was drinking, and how proud I felt to be in this farmhouse.

Below is the exact diary entry I wrote in November 2019 whilst at my NLP training.

"It's December 2020 and I'm sitting in our very own farmhouse with Champagne. I hear the sound of music playing but there is no other noise. I can see for miles across the fields, it's a beautiful view, undisturbed with not a single house in sight. It's so peaceful and calm. I feel so proud to have created this homely space. Ollie my horse and Kiwi my dog love living here, and Si is so much happier and relaxed. I am so grateful to have generated £250k in sales in 2020. I love our cream and oak kitchen and love my garden office. It has a luxurious, feminine feel to it. I love having friends stay in our spare rooms. The house smells so lovely thanks to my lime, basil, and mandarin candles. The beef is in the slow cooker, and we've got a lovely Christmas tree. It feels so perfect."

All of that became true. Although the garden office took much longer than planned, it is now finished! What is absolutely crazy is, I always have Christmas candles burning throughout December. When I wrote this in November 2019, I clearly forgot that and chose my year-round favourite of lime, basil & mandarin. In November 2020, I ordered my Christmas winter scent from The White Company, although the parcel went missing and we never had our Christmas 3-wick that we'd normally have. So in December 2020, the date of this diary entry, I reflected on what I had written, and despite it being nearly Christmas, was shocked that I did in fact have a lime, basil & mandarin candle burning. I hadn't read this diary entry since I had written it 13 months prior. In that time, we had been chosen as the successful new tenants of a Gloucestershire County Council farm, the exact one we wanted and the exact one I used to walk past with Kiwi, each time telling her we'll live here one day. We had absolutely no way of guaranteeing or knowing we'd get this exact farm. Hundreds of applicants apply for farms like this in our area, but this manifestation worked.

This exercise works well on a number of levels. Firstly, it stimulates the Reticular Activating System, your mind's own search engine. It also gives direction to the universe for your manifestation, and it lets you get clear on what you want to achieve, and how you'll feel when you achieve it. This enables your subconscious mind to give you the creative ideas and self-belief required to help it become your reality.

Literally, anything and everything can be designed. You've just got to put the time and intention in and totally take control of how you wish your day to go.

Task

- Write out your mission statement. Think about what you do, why you do it, and the impact you want to have in this world.
- Decide how you want your day to go. If you could write out an ideal day, what would that look like?
- What do you wish the non-negotiables of your day to be? Get clear on them, write them out, and design each day.
- Try this every morning for a month and notice the changes. The wonderful, positive, and intentional days will roll out just for you!
- Write out your future diary entry. It can be super basic, but clear on the senses, what you can see, smell, hear, feel, who you're with, and where you are. Just let yourself dream. Then put that notebook somewhere safe, remember the date or set a reminder in your phone and see what comes true!

CHAPTER 20

THE VARYING LENGTHS AND WAYS TO DO A MORNING ROUTINE

When I was first encouraged to do a morning routine, I remember telling my coach I didn't have time. She told me to make time. Stern, but such good advice. As I had her holding me accountable and regularly checking in, I knew I had to at least try. My goodness am I pleased I stuck with it.

Saying you don't have time is simply an excuse and actually a limiting belief. We all have the same 24 hours in a day, and I encourage you to consider how you spend yours. Being 'busy' is also an excuse. The choice really is yours - if you want to take control of how your day will go, work on your mindset, improve your self-belief and confidence, and therefore your life. Or do you want to fall out of bed and stay stuck? Most people want the former while doing the latter. This creates a massive disconnect between their actions and the progress they make forwards.

To change something within you takes time, grit, and determination. You've been a certain way for decades, now you want to shift your way of thinking, form better habits, and take control of your mind. It's a lot, and it's all possible. The issue is most people don't have staying power. They don't have accountability. They try something for a while then the desire disappears.

I know you are different. You haven't read this far to stop now. You haven't read this far not to take the action. I praise you for that. This book fell into your hands because you desire to change. All I ask of you is that you take action. Don't just read this book and then move on to the next book. Read this book, do the homework at the end of each chapter, and then start to witness the change in not only your mindset but your life.

It has truly changed my life. I was the one who said she didn't have time for a morning routine. I'm now known as the morning routine queen.

Hands on my heart, I do believe this to be possible for you too.

There are varying lengths of morning routines and I want you to find one that works for you.

First, I would recommend starting small with a short daily routine. It's much easier to form a new habit with small steps or in small chunks. If you want to start running, you're not going to go from 0 to 10k in two days. You start small and build on it. You start to enjoy it. It subconsciously becomes a new habit and then you build on it some more. You see the progress and the shifts, and it becomes easier. Your mind is a muscle in the same way that when you start exercising you start building muscles, and it then gets easier, the same applies to your mind. The more you exercise your mind, the stronger it gets, and the easier it is to maintain a certain standard.

Just a few years ago it was SO hard for me to get myself out of a funk, to believe in something, to change how my mind is wired. Now I can do it within minutes, sometimes even seconds. This is because I built up that muscle, gradually over time.

We've already discussed why doing the routine in the first hour of waking is so important, but I want to re-cap a little here.

In the first sixty minutes of your waking day, your mind is in the Theta state. This is a highly influential state where you can rewire and shape your mind. It's the point at which it's acting like a sponge, absorbing all that we tell it. This is a key opportunity in your day to get the most out of your mindset work. Spending ten minutes in this state will have much more of an impact than spending sixty minutes in a state of high alertness and focused on problem-solving. When your mind is in a state of high alert and problem-solving, it's actually at its highest level of consciousness.

If you recall, it is the subconscious part of the mind we wish to work with when making these changes, so trying to work on a subconscious level when the mind is at its highest level of consciousness is really not going to have the impact we desire.

I totally get that you'll still be busy or struggle to sit down for a whole hour, so I've broken it down into three varying lengths so there really is something for everyone! As I said, start small and build on it. When I started mine, I would spend approximately ten minutes on it, then it built up to twenty and is generally now twenty to thirty minutes a day.

Five Minutes

When I suggest spending five minutes on yourself and your mind, a lot of people brush the suggestion off because they don't feel it will do anything. Five minutes a day over the course of a year is 1,825 minutes, a whopping thirty hours!! Imagine the change that thirty hours of mindset work can make in your life!

Plus, it is the small regular activity that really makes a difference, over time, you'll be able to change your state and your mindset even quicker.

If you have five minutes, I suggest the following. I would set a timer for each of these 1-minute breakdowns to keep you laser focused and accountable to the time.

1 minute - Brain dump and journaling. Free and clear your mind, get everything out, even if "order dog food" is swimming around in the back of your mind, get it out on paper.

1 minute - Organise that list. Look at your priority activities, what needs to be done today, what doesn't really need to be done at all, what do you need support with, and what mindset work you need to do based on what came up.

1 minute - Gratitude rampage. Spend this time just being insanely grateful for everything! Your house, friends, family, your mind, your fingers that enable you to turn the pages in this book, your food and drink, your health, happiness, business, or career. Just spend one whole minute being grateful for anything and everything, this will really raise your vibration.

1 minute - Do your affirmations. Either write them out or say them but make sure you believe them and feel them! If you don't believe them when you say or write them, or you're just doing it to tick the box then it will make absolutely no difference. Remember, what you believe is what you achieve.

1 minute - Connect with your vision board and write out your goal as if it already happened. Again, believe that this goal is possible. How would you feel to already have hit that goal? When you look at the vision board, how will it feel to have what you desire?

And there you have it! Five focused minutes of mindset work that is going to help clear your mind, raise your vibration, solidify your beliefs, and keep you focused on your future! It really can be that easy, you simply have to do it.

The next step is to ensure you have those five minutes blocked out, and you are willing to commit to this as a habit. Your mind likes to clearly see things, which is where tracking the new habit can really help. This will give your mind physical evidence that you're doing something constructive. If you go to tarabest.com/book you will find a habit tracker that you can print out and keep a tally of your new habit creation. Examples of my vision boards can also be found there.

I also recommend giving yourself a small reward to celebrate milestones in your morning routine journey. You will most likely find that it's easy and enjoyable for a week or two, but then the enjoyment or desire may wear off. Studies show that the majority of people will give up. Please, please, please stick with it. I stand by a morning routine so fully because I know without a shadow of a doubt that it will change your life. As I said early on in this book, it takes at least 21 times for something to form a new habit. That's only three weeks of consistency. I would say about 90% of my clients will only manage to dip in and out in those first three weeks, and that's

OK. They have me holding them accountable and encouraging them to keep trying it.

To help you stay accountable I have actually created a Facebook group for readers of this book, so we can share our wins, challenges, stretches, and progress. Allow my team and me to hold you accountable, particularly in that first month.

Go to tarabest.com/book for the link to the Facebook group.

Remember, just five minutes a day can change your life. Simply making a commitment to try moves you so many steps ahead of the majority of the global population who may never bother to try.

Twenty Minutes

Twenty minutes a day is where I started my morning routine in October 2018. It felt really difficult. I resisted. I told my coach I didn't have the time. I found it really hard to create that habit. I felt like I was sitting there for 20 minutes doing nothing for the sake of saying I'd done it for that duration.

I carried on with that until my July 2019 meltdown when I felt stuck and completely broke. At that time, I really couldn't focus on all of the stages of the routine, so I did the steps that I felt would give me the best progress. I focused on journaling, gratitude, and affirmations. Once I started to see the progress in my mindset, my money, and my beliefs, I then went back up to a slightly longer one.

I can honestly say, since the pandemic struck in March 2020, I have consistently done a 15-30 minute morning routine and I truly love it more than ever. I feel more connected than ever before. I can hand on my heart say, the growth of my company and personal success in

CHAPTER 20

that year (and since then) was due to my morning routine and mindset.

A big change for me in that monumental year was actually connecting with my future self and the vision I had for my global company, rather than staying stuck in the now and worrying about the day-to-day and everything that was going on in the world. Watching the news and worrying wasn't going to do anything for my future, so I chose to focus on what I could control, and I stayed focused and aligned with my purpose and vision. When you're truly focused on your future and your bigger mission, you can't feel scarcity or lack for the now. Your mind really can't think or feel two emotions or two time frames at any one time. The majority of people will just stay stuck in the now or in the past, only thinking about their current reality or what life has been like thus far.

Again, I know you are different.

If you have twenty minutes available, I recommend the following:

3 minutes - Gratitude. Getting into a place of gratitude is one of the quickest and easiest ways to raise your vibration. Your mind can't feel apprehensive or like it's coming from a place of lack when you're feeling grateful, it just can't. As with the example shared in the one-minute section of the five-minute routine, find anything and everything to get yourself into that place. You can be grateful for your phone, fresh flowers, blue skies, your best friend, your pet, or the pure fact that you're willing to see things differently and create a better life for yourself. If you have something exciting on that day, I also recommend doing a forward gratitude. A forward gratitude is where you're basically being grateful for something going as well as it possibly can. As an example, if I had a call with a potential client, my morning routine gratitude would be around how grateful I am that I'm speaking to an absolute dream client, who I know is excited to create her dream life, is excited to say yes to her success, willing to invest, and sees the benefit in doing so. I would practice being grateful for her signing up before I even speak to her, as this would not only mentally prepare me but also send a really strong message to the universe.

3 minutes - Affirmations. I actually love to set a timer and write out affirmations for three minutes solid. It really does raise my vibration and energy and helps me to realise anything is possible. It helps me get into the state of how I wish to be and feel, and again, keeps me so focused on my goal of how I wish to live and show up. The really important thing here is that you *feel* them. Writing them out for the sake of ticking the box really won't make that much of a difference. Believe that it is possible for you because what you believe is what you achieve!

2 minutes - Vision board. Your vision board is another great tool to help you connect to your future. As previously suggested, I recommend focusing on 3-5 pictures per morning, just so that you can really connect to them. I feel it's better to fully connect with a couple of them than try to feel the feelings of all of them. Obviously, you want to do what works best for you, so try it and see what fits.

2 minutes - Connecting to your next goal and writing it out. Before and during writing this book, I did a lot of research on goals, analysing what helps people hit them, how many people set them, and what holds them back from hitting them. There were a large variety of answers, but the underlying message was that people don't set goals because they don't feel like they can achieve them.

They don't have accountability, or they don't know which goals to set. If this is you, go back to chapter 13, set yourself a small goal to work towards, and incorporate it into your morning routine. Believe you can hit it, feel the feelings of hitting it, and stay connected and focused on it.

5 minutes - Journaling. We have more going on in our minds than ever before, we know this by now. Our minds are coping with and processing more than ever before and we're expecting them to run as normal. Which includes managing our lives and being instantly available for us, while making them more online and present than ever before. Make sure you do your bit to support your mind, by freeing it up in the mornings. Get everything out of it so you can arrange it as you desire for your day ahead. Know it is there to support you and grow with you. So often I hear people say they don't know what to write when it comes to journaling. Trust yourself, put pen to paper and see what comes out. Just let it flow. That's where setting the timer works really well because it will encourage you to just free-write. You may be surprised by what comes up, just let it be. It needs to come up for a reason so just allow it. If five minutes feels too big for you, try starting with just one minute, then gradually increase the time. The more I practise journaling the easier it gets. I use it to clear my mind, connect with my future self, and decide how I wish my day, week, or month to go. Do what feels right for you.

5 minutes - Meditating. The art of meditation is simply to quiet the mind. We are all SO busy and online more than ever so it's a great tool to actually give yourself some peace and quiet. There are many amazing and short guided meditations on YouTube, head to tarabest.com/book for the link to my YouTube Meditation playlist and to listen to the guided meditation I've created. Spending just five minutes a day meditating will help you feel calmer and more focused for the day. Simply focus on your breathing and clearing your mind.

There is no specific order to do these. If you feel you have a lot on your plate and going on in your mind, it might be best to journal first to get those thoughts out, and then do your gratitude's, affirmations, and so on to get yourself into a great place. If you're already feeling great, then the order above will work wonders. This is the order I do them in.

Sixty Minutes

When you've committed to the 20-minute routine, you will likely find that you really enjoy it. I love mine now, but it did take time to get to that point. The more you start to love it, the more you might find you have even more to say or that you want to take it to the next level. Below is a guide for a 60-minute morning routine, but you may take parts of this one and create your own if you have only 30 or 45 minutes.

I do a 60-minute morning routine on a handful of occasions. Firstly, if I've been away and need to get my head back in the game and connected to the work I do. Secondly, if I'm feeling really overwhelmed, I use my morning routine as a way of clearing out overwhelm and getting myself into a great place. And lastly, if I'm launching something in my business. My launches require a lot of energy, a super mindset, and lots of connection. So my morning routine would be around showing up, connecting with dream clients, and really building those lifelong relationships with my audience. Tune in to how you're feeling and give yourself the time, especially if you recognise that you need it.

5 minutes - Gratitude. This will really raise your energy and vibration! I challenge you to truly feel grateful for five minutes and feel amazing. Set a timer and get in the zone. Alternatively, you can set a timer and see how long you can find things to be grateful for. There is an unlimited amount of things to be grateful for, how many can you think of? Look around for inspiration.

5 minutes - Affirmations. Again, a good five-minute stint of positive and powerful "I am" statements will really raise your energy. Truly feel them and think big, way outside of the box. If you could write a character for yourself, how would you describe her?

15 minutes - Journaling. Such an important part of the morning routine and a key space to clear your head. If you missed it, I do encourage you to go back to chapter 11 and read how journaling can help you. I have clients who literally journal as part of their morning routine and don't rely on anything else. It helps to clear their mind, connect to what they're working towards, and helps them be their biggest fan. It's like clearing the canvas of the mind ahead of the day, then feeding it with what you desire. All the thoughts and things that will help you create what you desire to create.

5 minutes - Setting the intention for the day and visualising how you wish for it to go. A lot of people don't actually choose or decide how they want their day to go. They just let it happen. Taking control first thing in the morning by writing out how you wish for your day to go will set the tone and intention. Consider if you have meetings, a deadline, or a large project, how do you want it to feel, how do you want it to go, and write out in advance how it will happen. I'll bet you'd write that it went perfectly, you remained calm, in control and focused, you had the desired outcome, and everything felt so natural and came from a place of ease. Write that! Then connect to it and feel the feelings, then watch it unravel, rather than just letting it happen without being prepared. I love to do this for calls I have with potential clients - I write out how perfectly they go, I get really clear on my energy, the takeaways that particular person has, and how they respond to me and my programmes. More often than not, the call happens exactly as I write it. Start creating your dream life!

15 minutes - Reading. I really love reading however, it wasn't until 2018 that I started to read books about business. Before that, my days were at full intensity and the last thing I wanted to do was read about business. I wanted to escape in a heartwarming rom com book. Now, I love to read and have found great comfort in many books. You can find a list of my favourites at tarabest.com/book.

Your mind is like a muscle. Reading is a great way to exercise it and keep it alert, whether you're into mindset or business books, a good fictional rom com, or a thrilling novel, do what feels good for you and brings you enjoyment.

10 minutes - Move your body. There are many ways you can move your body, from yoga and pilates to exercise and dancing. I love to stretch and dance when I want to raise my vibration and get myself into a great energy and vibe. Yoga is a great way to quiet the mind, much like meditation. I will admit, I don't do yoga, however, I have clients that do and swear by it as part of their mindset work. As with the morning routine, start small, perhaps using a YouTube video as guidance, and just remember, even 5-10 minutes a day will offer benefits to your body and mind.

10 minutes - Energy work. Getting yourself into the right energy for your day and what you wish to attract. This will vary depending on your mood. You might wish to raise your energy because you're really tired, in which case a short workout, playing some of your favourite music nice and loud, or having a dance party will help. If you feel like you're coming from a place of lack one morning, the energy work might be releasing those feelings and getting yourself into a space of abundance.

As I said, I would suggest starting small. Be kind to yourself, and start to get a feel for what supports your progress. And then, celebrate! Champagne is optional but encouraged!

CHAPTER 21

A HEARTFELT CONGRATULATIONS!

I must commend you on getting to the end! Studies show 63% of readers don't finish a book so you're already ahead of the game!

I hope this book has inspired you to think about how you start your day, and how you can set yourself up for success. You really can create your dream life and future. It starts in your mind. It starts with you making the decision, committing to it, and then holding yourself accountable. Accountability can be a hard thing to maintain and master so I would love to invite you over to my private Facebook group where you can share your key takeaways and perhaps use it as a platform for accountability and to connect with others on this journey. Simply head to www.tarabest.com/book for the link to join.

I understand it might feel overwhelming, and it's intimidating to start a new habit, but let me ask you this…